Consider

HOMESCHOOLING

Enjoy!

Cari

Cari Kelemen

ISBN: 978-1-7372016-0-1

Library of Congress Control Number: 2021910258

Book design by Cari Kelemen

Printed by DiggyPOD, Inc., in the United States of America

Published by Books by Cari, Dallas, Texas

booksbycari.com

To my husband
Russ
and our children
Cooper, Cassie, and Catie.
Thank you for going on this
homeschool adventure
with me.
I love you all.

Contents

foreword

"Have you ever considered homeschooling?" she asked.

My wife and I were grappling with the dilemma that almost every parent wrestles with as soon as their first child is born—what to do about their education? There were several boxes we were hoping to check as we searched for a school:

We wanted a school that would encourage the healthy pair-bond between our daughters, just eighteen months apart, and that would allow them to stay together in the same grade at least for the first year. This eliminated the public schools.

We wanted a school with a small enough student body so our daughters might have the same classmates year after year and the possibility of forming lifelong friendships.

We wanted a school that emphasized the importance of hand work, household work, and unstructured play.

And we needed a school close enough to my workplace so I could quickly respond in the event of an emergency, and that was in or near a neighborhood with homes we could afford.

Even while our family was still growing and there were major logistics to work out, we secured our spot for the upcoming school year at our favorite pick with a hefty deposit.

In this backdrop, I recall having a lengthy conversation with my friend, Cari Kelemen. As she listened carefully, she picked up on both my anxiety to find the best school I could, and the sadness I was feeling that my girls were rapidly approaching school age and would soon be leaving our home for the majority of their day.

She helped me see that the patterns we were drawn to in our school choices already occur naturally in the home. Unconsciously, we were trying to do our best to create an artificial "home away from home" for our children, except for the one major material difference.

"But in their 'new home,' you and your wife won't be there," she pointed out. "Other adults will be."

This was my eureka moment. It sparked a new question that I've grappled with ever since. What is this ineffable ability these other adults have, beyond the ability of the actual parents, to train up our children to the highest standards? I could not come up with an adequate answer.

So we decided to school our children at home. This allowed us to transition to a single-income family, leave our densely urban area and find an affordable home in a supportive community where homeschooling is embraced.

And here is what I've learned along the way: with a modicum of effort, you can provide a top-notch education—and upbringing!—for your child, and your family will be well-rewarded for doing so.

Not a day goes by that I do not count my blessings for the home environment we have managed to put into order. We spent money upfront to ensure we had the materials we needed to support the daily schedule. I could not have imagined it, but adding it all up, including the ongoing costs to date, the sum total has not even put a dent in the initial deposit that was refunded to us years ago.

What's priceless is that our children are secure, strong, self-reliant, and cheerful. They have many friends and are ready to provide help to others if needed. Another bonus is that they far outpace all academic benchmarks for children their age. In fact, we have not identified a single downside to educating our children at home.

My hope is that you find Cari's case for homeschooling as persuasive as I did. Much of what we discussed is included in this book. Perhaps while you read it, you will have a eureka moment of your own.

– Ray Botty, *Cari's homeschooling friend*

Consider

HOMESCHOOLING

introduction

His eyes narrowed.

"You want to what?"

"I think I want to homeschool our children."

I figured we'd be on two different pages. He is a "Teacher of the Year" award-winning public school teacher who holds a master's degree in education administration. And I was a stay-at-home mom with three preschoolers.

"Why?" he asked.

It was a simple, valid question, but it took numerous conversations with him to answer it. Understandably, my husband wanted to know where in the world I had gotten such an idea, and why I felt confident enough to try it.

Like most people, my idea of "school" was based on my own educational experience which took place in both public and private school classrooms. Most of my teachers were wonderful, and I made decent grades, but as a student, I was just not well-suited for a classroom. It wasn't until I began to plan for the education of my own children that I became aware there was an alternative.

Since you have picked up this book, I would wager that, for your own reasons, you are looking for an alternative too. You are ready to re-examine, rethink, and reimagine what education traditionally looks like, and to consider if homeschooling might be a good fit for your children and your family.

That's why I'm here.

Before we begin, I want to make two clarifications: first, when I use the term "homeschooling" I am not referring to remote or virtual education, or any other type of classroom-at-home. Homeschooling is a parent-involved, home-based, non-classroom form of education that more closely resembles private tutoring.

Second, this book is for those who are exploring the educational options for their children's current or future education. It is not intended for those who already chose a different path. My goal is not to make anyone second guess past decisions but to simply make the case for homeschooling as a viable option.

This is not so much a how-to, but a why-to homeschool book. As I've talked to family, friends, and other parents about homeschooling, I've noticed many of the same questions keep popping up. I will specifically address those questions, as well the seeds that were planted in my mind along the way that inspired me to look into homeschooling, long before I was even a parent.

As you consider homeschooling and as you read this book, my hope is, at least once, you will say to yourself, "I've never thought of it that way before."

one

Who Will Be Making Your Child's First Impressions?

"You never get a second chance to make a first impression."

– Will Rogers

There was a collective audible gasp in the room followed by scattered whispers. I was at a meeting for mothers of young children, ages birth through age five called MOPS (Mothers of Preschoolers). The leader had just announced the topic of the speaker for our next meeting: why you should talk to your child about sex before they go to kindergarten.

*Wait…**what**? That can't be right,* I said to myself. *That's way too young. Isn't "The Talk" something you're supposed to have when your child is much, much older?*

After the meeting, I picked up my one-year-old firstborn from the nursery and looked at his sweet chubby face.

This is all happening way too fast.

The speaker, Mary Flo Ridley, was another mom who was passionate about this topic and who was becoming a widely-known and sought-after speaker. She immediately calmed our apprehensions by telling our MOPS group that she was *not* advising us to have a full-blown, detailed sex talk with our preschoolers. But she *was* advocating simple, age-appropriate, factual snippets of information, given when your child naturally expresses curiosity. Detailed facts can come later; the important thing is to impart your own values to your child *first* before someone else does.

Mary Flo waited for teachable moments with her preschool-aged daughter, and through short, ongoing conversations, her daughter learned a few simple things about sex that reflected her parents' beliefs: sex is God's gift to marriage, it's how husbands and wives have a baby, and it should be kept private.

She asked us to imagine a dry sponge in the mind of our child that represents his curiosity about sexual things. As his parent, you have the opportunity to fill it first with what you think is important for him to know. You have the power of the first impression. If you have already satisfied his curiosity with what you think is of value and importance, then other information he encounters on the topic just kind of rolls off. But if, out of a sense of protecting him from the subject, you never talk with him about it, you have left him wide open to absorb whatever a peer or the culture has to say about it. And then *they*, not *you*, will have the power of the first impression.

She encouraged us to be the first to fill our children's curiosity sponge before they went to school, because even though your child's kindergarten classroom is full of five-year-olds, not every five-year-old comes from similar home environments. Your five-year-old may be the firstborn in your home, with a toddler and a baby for siblings, and most of your music and entertainment are geared for a five-year-old.

But the kindergartener sitting next to your child may be the youngest of four in her home, where the oldest sibling is sixteen, and the music and other entertainment are geared for a teenager. And most children "in the know" are usually all too happy to share their knowledge with less enlightened children.

Then Mary Flo told us a story I'll never forget. Her five-year-old daughter had just made a new friend at kindergarten whose teenage brother was in charge of watching her after school.

"I don't think you will ever let me go over to play at her house." she told her mother.

"Why not?"

Her daughter answered, "Because after school she watches her brother and his girlfriend have sex."

Mary Flo quickly closed her gaping jaw and tried to disguise her own shock. Fortunately, she was able to sound calm.

"And why do you think you shouldn't do that?" she pursued.

"Well," she paused, "you told me that sex is for husbands and wives—and they aren't married. And you said it was private, so I know we shouldn't be watching."

Wow. Mary Flo had been the first to satisfy her daughter's curiosity with her own values, and the power of that first impression protected her daughter from a very inappropriate situation.

Our MOPS group left the meeting with the resolve to follow Mary Flo's example with our own kids. And those of us with three and four-year-olds seemed well aware that time was already running short.

As I left the meeting and mulled over what I had heard, there were a couple of things nagging at me. The first was this huge clock hanging over my head as a parent, *ticking, ticking, ticking*, down to the dreaded deadline of age five —the year when you are supposed to enroll your child in a school.

Why age five? Who decided that age five was the point in time when my part as my child's primary teacher was mostly done, and now it's time for the professional teachers to take the reins? Something about it didn't seem right. Age five didn't feel like it gave me enough time with my child. I was already feeling rushed, and it just didn't sit right with my soul.

I remember talking with a neighbor who felt the same way. She attended a church that also had an elementary school. One Sunday the principal of the school reminded her it was time to enroll her daughter in kindergarten.

"I'm just not ready yet," she told him.

"But she's five," he stated flatly.

"Exactly," she said. "She's just *five*."

Is the sadness in the gut of a parent who sends their child off on their first day of school just a sign they need to let go? Or is there something else possibly telling that parent that something about this situation isn't right for them or their child?

The other thought nagging at me was that Mary Flo's curiosity sponge only dealt with one subject matter. What about all of the other areas of curiosity in my child's mind on all kinds of different subjects? Who was going to be first to fill those?

It was easy to envision that if I sent my kids to a traditional classroom, I could be put on the defense as a parent. What if some of their first impressions needed to be undone? Is that even possible? There's no way I wanted *my* values to be the ones that just kind of rolled off of my kids. Nope. *I* wanted to be the one on offense.

As I considered home schooling, I knew who I wanted to have the time and opportunity to make most of my kids' first impressions— me.

Cari and the kids

two

What Should I Expect from My Kids?

"Nobody rises to low expectations."

– Calvin Lloyd

As we've seen, first impressions can have a tremendous impact on our children, but there is another tool at our disposal as parents that is so powerful, it doesn't even have to be spoken aloud in order for it to have immense influence —our expectations.

Before I was married, I attended a conference called "The Seven Laws of the Learner" taught by a man named Dr. Bruce Wilkinson. Bruce told a story about when he was a first-year professor at a college in Oregon. There were eight sections of a mandatory freshman course with about thirty students in each one. Bruce was assigned to teach sections one, two, and three. Before the semester began, he ran in to an older professor on campus.

"How in the world did you get assigned section two?" he asked Bruce. "I have sections six, seven, and eight and I've been here longer."

"What's section two?"

"It's the most coveted class on the entire campus. It's where they place all of the best students, the cream of the crop of the entire freshman class, in one room. It's going to be as different as night and day—the interaction, the quality of their papers… you're going to just feel the excitement. The electricity is going to be bouncing off the walls. It's going to be unbelievable! I can't believe they gave it to *you!*"

On the first day of class, Bruce taught section one, and it went great. But the instant the section two students came into the classroom, he could easily tell what the older faculty member was talking about. He could feel the energy crackling in the air. The class discussion moved along so easily and so well; it was over before he knew it. As the semester went on, he always found himself looking forward to teaching section two.

About halfway through the semester, the academic dean asked him how things were going.

"It's going great! I'm especially enjoying section two!"

"Is it really that different?"

"Oh, yes!" Then Bruce described in detail all the ways section two was superior as a class to sections one and three.

"That's interesting," he said, "because we cancelled section two this year. We spread the outstanding students evenly among all eight sections."

No! That can't be right! Dumbfounded, Bruce went to his office to find a way to prove him wrong. He checked his grade book to see what kind of grades he had given sections one and three, and they were pretty average. And then he looked at the grades he had given section two: A, A-, B+, A, A+, A... he was simply stunned.

Then he saw a stack of papers the students had written that he hadn't graded yet. He laid all three stacks next to each other on his desk. Section one and section three combined were not as high as the stack of the papers from section two—same assignment. Section two had way outperformed their peers by writing longer papers. He couldn't believe this was happening!

What was different between the three sections of his students? Absolutely nothing. It was the same day of the week, the same teacher, the same outline, the same freshmen students ... the only difference was in his head. The difference wasn't in the students, it was in their teacher—it was in his *mind*. The conversation he had with that older faculty member before the semester began set his expectations higher for section two, and astoundingly, without the students knowing a thing about it, they responded to his higher expectations.

But what would have happened if Bruce had been told that section three was where the outstanding students had been placed? Would *they* have outperformed sections one and two? Most certainly. What we think privately in our minds about others has an enormous effect on how they respond to us. Without even a single word spoken, people have an uncanny tendency to live up to, or down to, our expectations of them.

Bruce's story left a huge impression on me. I started to become acutely aware of other people's expectations of me, and my expectations of them. And since they can be impactful in both positive and negative ways, I've tried to set positive expectations for myself and others. I've actually begun to see a low expectation for someone as a form of disrespect, and a high expectation as an act of love. According to scripture's "love chapter," often recited at weddings, "If you love someone you will… always expect the best of him." 1 Corinthians 13:7

The power of a loving expectation has played out in my own family. My three children are the same gender and birth order as my family of origin with almost identical spacing. My youngest daughter, Catie, is in my old spot. My mom had an older friend named Edith, who had three children, and she said something very interesting to my mother when she was pregnant with me.

"Oh, you're going to enjoy this third child so much," Edith told her.

When my mother asked her why, she gave her all kinds of reasons: you're already broken-in as a parent, you already have a boy, you already have a girl, and this third "bonus child" is just going to be a delight—a pure joy.

"And you were," my mom later told me.

Did Edith elevate my mother's expectations about raising a third child? Did I unknowingly respond to the unspoken expectations of my mother? Perhaps. And even though I never said it out loud, I privately expected Catie to be a delightful joy as well. And she was.

When I began to imagine my future children's education in a traditional classroom setting, I wondered: Will their teachers have high or low expectations for their students? Will my child's teacher have a high or low expectation of my child in particular? How will their teacher's expectations of them influence their behavior?

As I considered homeschooling, there was one person I knew who would lovingly and consistently have high expectations of my kids— me.

Delightful Catie

three

Who Do You Want to Guide Your Child's Discoveries?

"People generally see what they look for, and hear what they listen for."

— *Harper Lee*

A few years ago, a friend of mine expressed disappointment that she rarely heard the phrase "Merry Christmas" anymore—that it had been replaced by "Happy Holidays" or "Season's Greetings." I wondered if her sentiment was true, so I decided to listen for it while I was Christmas shopping. After paying at the first store, the clerk smiled at me.

"Merry Christmas," she said.

"Thank you, Merry Christmas to you," I replied.

Well, there's one, I thought, *and I was not the first to say it.*

Next, while I was at the post office buying Christmas stamps, I got it again.

"Merry Christmas," said the attendant.

"Merry Christmas," I said back. I wondered, *Did she just say that to me because I was buying stamps with "Merry Christmas" on them?* Maybe.

But after several more stops, I heard the phrase "Merry Christmas" several other times being exchanged by store clerks and shared between customers. Whose reality was right? Mine or my friend's? Was "Merry Christmas" being said more often, or did I just hear it more because I was listening for it?

Have you ever noticed a certain make and model of a car at a traffic light and wondered if you should look into it as your next car? Then, all of the sudden, that make and model of car seems to be all over the place, almost everywhere you look! Are there really more of that type of car on the roads, or are you just now noticing them?

People tend to find what they're looking for. Why? Because they're looking for it! And in a way similar to setting expectations, you can guide what people find by suggesting what they look for.

Guiding what people look for is the idea behind gratitude journals. The concept is to begin each day looking for something new for which to be grateful and then write it in your journal at night. And it works! People who spend their day on the lookout for something to be grateful for will invariably find it.

It's a wonderful thing when what you're looking for is positive, like a fortune inside a fortune cookie, but it can work in negative ways too. Let's say you are looking forward to seeing a movie based on the recommendation of a friend, but before you go, you see a movie review that expresses disappointment with how it ends. So now, as you watch the entire movie, instead of simply enjoying it, you are on the lookout for reasons to be disappointed with the ending.

With children, a parent's guidance in what to look for can greatly shape their experiences. Imagine parents in a parking lot, telling their kids goodbye and putting them on a bus to summer camp. One set of parents looks anxious and worried and goes over with their kid, one more time, what to do when he gets homesick. Another set of parents looks excited and happy and tells their child how much fun she's going to have, and how many new things she'll get to do, and how many new friends she's going to make. Which child do you think is going to have a better time at camp?

In a classroom setting, what is a student being guided to look for? What are they looking for in their country's past, in their science books, or in themselves? What will their peers guide them to look for? What do you want them to find?

As I considered homeschooling, I knew someone who really wanted the chance to guide my children's discoveries— me.

The Kelemen kiddos

four

Will My Kids Really Be Able to Learn from Home?

"There is no school equal to a decent home and no teacher equal to a virtuous parent."

– Mahatma Gandhi

I was recently seated on a plane next to two girls in their mid-twenties who were on their way to a bachelorette weekend for a friend who was getting married. I told them I was doing research for a book and asked them where they went to high school. They both attended public high schools. Then I asked them to tell me about their most memorable educational experience. One recalled an out-of-town robotics competition, and the other one said it was a trip with the marching band. My secret guess was right—neither one mentioned an educational experience that happened inside the classroom.

One of my most memorable educational experiences in high school didn't happen in the classroom either. My dad had a business trip to New York City and because I'd never been there, I convinced him to take me with him. We added in a college visit so I could get an excused absence. Who knows what I missed at school that week—I certainly don't remember. But I'll never forget that trip.

I got to see a musical on Broadway, visit some great restaurants, and see some iconic sights. But my favorite day was when my dad dropped me off at The Metropolitan Museum of Art for several hours while he attended a meeting. I was taking an art class at the time, and I thought The Met was heaven. There was so much ground to cover, but I just couldn't bring myself to simply breeze through the rooms and merely glance at the paintings. Instead, I stood in front of each one for several minutes, trying to absorb it before I moved on to the next.

One of the museum guides noticed what I was doing and asked me why I was taking my time. I told him about my art class and how much I loved it. Coincidentally, he was working towards a degree in art history and was excited to share what he was learning. In his area of the museum, he led me on a mini-tour and told me the stories behind the artists, the message they were trying to convey with their subject matter, and all about the compositions and techniques. I got my own personal art lecture at The Met!

But the lasting lesson is this: any place can be your classroom, and anyone can be your teacher. Everyone you meet can teach you something you didn't already know.

Our homeschool got a whole new group of teachers when we renovated our house. I took my kids with me everywhere during the process —from City Hall to apply with the Board of

Adjustment, to the office of City Planning and Zoning to map out a new plat line, and to the architect's office to draw it all up. Our construction foreman was terrific with kids and answered all of their questions. They got to see firsthand why knowing math is important!

When it was all over, we took a plate of cookies to an office of city employees who were especially helpful. My daughter handed them a crayon drawing of our house with a big "Thank you!" written at the top. One of them slipped it into a plastic sleeve and attached it to the side of a filing cabinet that is visible from the front desk. The last time I checked, years later, it was still there. We met so many interesting people with fascinating jobs and learned to appreciate all that it takes to make a big city run.

Which leads me to the question: when did we, as a society, start limiting "learning environments" to a classroom? When you look at the history of education, the classroom model as we know it is relatively new. Education through the centuries has been both formal and informal, and it has included everything from one-on-one apprenticeships to small groups of disciples. But the most common form of education for most people throughout history has been within the home and within the family.

There is an ancient text from the Old Testament where parents are instructed how to teach their children:

> And you must think constantly about these commandments I am giving you today. You must teach them to your children and talk about them when you are at home or out for a walk; at bedtime and the first thing in the morning. Tie them on your finger, wear them on your forehead, and write them on the doorposts of your house! Deuteronomy 6:6-9

In this context, it is the parents who have the ultimate responsibility to teach their own children. And the lessons are part of their lifestyle—they happen anywhere, any time of day, as life is being lived out.

Today, homeschooling may sound new, but it's really a return to the way most people have been educated. There have been times in history when all children were homeschooled—they learned in the context of their homes with their extended families that included multiple generations. They learned to work with the guidance of adults of all ages and played with other children of all ages.

And just to help put homeschooling in historical perspective, here are some people you might recognize who were homeschooled in full or in part:

US Presidents

George Washington
Abraham Lincoln
John Adams
John Quincy Adams
Grover Cleveland
James Garfield
William H. Harrison

Andrew Jackson
Thomas Jefferson
James Madison
Franklin D. Roosevelt
Theodore Roosevelt
John Tyler
Woodrow Wilson

Political Leaders

Winston Churchill
Alexander Hamilton
Patrick Henry
William Penn
Thomas Paine
Daniel Webster

Davy Crockett
Sam Houston
William J. Bryan
Susan B. Anthony
Sandra D. O'Connor
Condoleezza Rice

Military Leaders

Alexander the Great
Robert E. Lee
Stonewall Jackson

Douglas MacArthur
George Patton

Authors

Charles Dickens
C. S. Lewis
J. R. R. Tolkien
Mark Twain
Robert Frost
Agatha Christie
Beatrix Potter
Hans Christian An-
derson
Lewis Carroll
Jane Austen

George Bernard Shaw
Walt Whitman
Robert Browning
Robert Louis Steven-
son
Louisa May Alcott
Laura Ingalls Wilder
Virginia Woolf
Alex Haley
Carl Sandburg
William F. Buckley, Jr.

Scientists and Medical Leaders

Isaac Newton
Albert Einstein
Booker T. Washington
George Washinton
Carver

Blaise Pascal
Pierre Curie
Albert Schweitzer
Clara Barton
Florence Nightingale

Inventors

Alexander G. Bell
Benjamin Franklin
Thomas Edison

Eli Whitney
Orville & Wilbur
Wright

Businessmen

Andrew Carnegie
Ray Croc,
(McDonald's)
Dave Thomas,
(Wendy's)

Colonel Harland
Sanders, (KFC)
Joseph Pulitzer,
(Pulitzer Prize)

Religious Leaders

Joan of Arc
William Carey
Jonathan Edwards
Philipp Melanchthon

Dwight L. Moody
John Newton
John Owen
Hudson Taylor
John & Charles Wesley

Artists and Others

Leonardo da Vinci
Claude Monet
Rembrandt
Ansel Adams
Frank Lloyd Wright

Martha Washington
Abigail Adams
Helen Keller
Charlotte Mason
Amelia Earhart

Musicians

Wolfgang A. Mozart
Felix Mendelssohn
John Philip Sousa
Noel Coward
Irving Berlin
Louis Armstrong
The Jonas Brothers

Hanson
Barlow Girl
LeAnne Rimes
Taylor Swift
Justin Bieber
Justin Timberlake
Christina Aguilera

Entertainers

Charlie Chaplin
Will Rogers
Alan Alda
Whoopi Goldberg
Jennifer Love Hewitt
Hilary Duff

Ryan Gosling
Selena Gomez
Emma Watson
Elijah Woods
Dakota Fanning
Kristen Stewart

Athletes

Justin Jackson
Blake Griffin
Tim Tebow
Jason Taylor
Michelle Kwan
Serena Williams
Venus Williams
Maria Sharapova

Simone Biles
Misty Copeland
Bethany Hamilton
Shaun White
Bode Miller
Sage Kotsenburg
Joey Logano

I wonder, could the broadness of the accomplishments of these people be attributed to the broadness of their "classrooms?"

As I considered homeschooling, and studied the history of all the different ways children have been taught through the years, it became clear who was ultimately responsible for teaching mine— me.

The Kelemen family on an Easter Sunday

five

Shouldn't Teaching Be Left to the Experts?

"Who's to say who's an expert?"

— *Paul Newman*

In 2010, The Onion, a satirical news site, published an article titled "Increasing Number of Parents Opting to Have Children School-Homed." Here are some excerpts:

WASHINGTON—According to a report released Monday by the U.S. Department of Education, an increasing number of American parents are choosing to have their children raised at school rather than at home.

"Parents are finding creative ways to make this increasingly common child-rearing track work," said Deputy Education Secretary Anthony W. Miller. "Whether it's over-relying on after-school programs and extracurricular activities, or simply gross neglect, school-homing is becoming a widely accepted method of bringing children up."

Most said that an alarming number of legal guardians such as themselves lack the most basic common sense required to give children the type of instruction they need during crucial developmental years.

"It's really a matter of who has more experience in dealing with my child," Cincinnati resident Kevin Dufrense said of his decision to have his 10-year-old son Jake, school-homed. "These teachers are dealing with upwards of 40 students in their classrooms at a time, so obviously they know a lot more about children than someone like me, who only has one son and doesn't know where he is half the time anyway."

"Simply put, it's not the job of parents to raise these kids," Dufrense added.

I laughed out loud when I read this satire, but things that are funny always have an element of truth. In very real ways, we have gone from homeschooling to school-homing. In Massachusetts during the 1850s, parents resisted compulsory education by literally standing in their doorways, their children behind them, with muskets in hand. Now, school programs will feed your child breakfast, lunch, and after-school snacks. How did we go from "Don't take my child!" to "How long can you take my child?" And when did we decide that professional teachers, not the parents, are the experts when it comes to teaching our own kids?

There are two components to education: *what* is being taught and *who* is being taught.

There are many talented teachers who are experts on *what* is being taught, BUT when it comes to *who* is being taught—your own kids— ***you*** are the world's leading expert!

Much of what a professional teacher is trained to do is specifically geared for teaching in a classroom setting. When my husband was working on his master's degree in education, he was surprised by how much of the curriculum and class discussion was devoted to how to maintain behavioral order, or basically, crowd control. Many teachers will tell you that the amount of time spent in actual instruction is often less than the time it takes to capture and maintain their students' attention. Keeping students focused is a constant challenge. And no wonder—they're sitting in a room full of their peers!

When my oldest, Cooper, was ready to begin kindergarten, I purchased a curriculum from a reputable private school that "repackaged" their classroom curriculum for homeschoolers. They didn't do a very good job.

The very first thing in the lesson plan was an "attention getter." I looked at Cooper who was quietly sitting at the breakfast table next to me.

Why do I need an attention getter? I thought. *He's sitting there looking at me!*

Back in the box it went.

In contrast to classrooms, homeschooling allows the parents the luxury of focusing on their individual children. What makes them curious? How often do they need a break? What is their dominant learning style?

I didn't know what my own learning style was until I was pursuing my master's degree and took a class called Teaching Methods. The professor explained that the four main learning styles are the following:

auditory – learn by listening

visual – learn by seeing

kinetic – learn by doing

social – learn by discussing

It's not surprising that the traditional lecture-oriented classroom is geared specifically for auditory learners. But a thoughtful teacher will try to address all of the learning styles.

To illustrate the differences, we were instructed to get up and go to the corner of the classroom marked with our learning style. After several minutes, the professor smiled with satisfaction.

"Stop. Now look at yourselves. What are you doing?" he said. "Now look around the room. What are your classmates doing?"

The auditory learners were sitting quietly, listening for the next set of instructions. The visual learners were jotting down notes, some complete with a diagram of which learning style was in which corner of the room. The kinetic learners were physically moving their desks to accommodate the new arrangement of people. And the social learners were busy mixing and mingling with one another, like they were having a cocktail party without the cocktails.

As we all looked around the room at each other, we burst out laughing. The learning styles were dead on. I was at the "Social Learner's Meet & Greet." Ever since I was a child, whenever I learned something new, I wanted to talk about it. My favorite part of class was almost always the discussion. No wonder my first-grade teacher gave me a "U" for unsatisfactory in classroom decorum with the explanation "talks too much." I had to have a little moment of mourning for my six-year-old self who got punished for her learning style. (I still love you, Mrs. Gardner.)

I'm glad I knew about the learning styles before I began to homeschool. My middle child, Cassie, was KINETIC in all caps! She was wiggly in the womb; she was wiggly when you held her. She didn't walk, she bounced, and when she ran, she made big circles with one arm. But she was smart as a whip. When she began to read at age four, she would start by sitting next to me on the sofa, with the book in her lap. By the end of the book, she was twisted around, laying on her back holding the book over her head with her feet on the back of the sofa. But as her mother, I didn't care. She read the book perfectly! So, we celebrated. And I didn't once tell her to sit still.

A wiggly child, like Cassie, would not have been a good fit for a classroom. Neither was an English girl born in London in 1925. Her story is included in YouTube's most-viewed Ted Talk of all time titled "Do Schools Kill Creativity?" by Sir Ken Robinson:

I'm doing a new book at the moment called "Epiphany," which is based on a series of interviews with people about how they discovered their talent. I'm fascinated by how people got to be there. It's really prompted by a conversation I had with a wonderful woman who maybe most people have never heard of; she's called Gillian Lynne—have you heard of her? Some have. She's a choreographer and everybody knows her work. She did "Cats" and "Phantom of the Opera." She's wonderful.

Gillian and I had lunch one day and I said, "Gillian, how'd you get to be a dancer?"

And she said it was interesting; when she was at school, she was really hopeless. And the school, in the '30s, wrote to her parents and said, "We think Gillian has a learning disorder."

She couldn't concentrate; she was fidgeting. I think now they'd say she had ADHD. Wouldn't you? But this was the 1930s, and ADHD hadn't been invented at this point. It wasn't an available condition. People weren't aware they could have that.

Anyway, she went to see this specialist ... and she sat on her hands for twenty minutes while this man talked to her mother about all the problems Gillian was having at school. And at the end of it—because she was disturbing people; her homework was always late; and so on, little kid of eight—in the end, the doctor went and sat next to Gillian and said, "Gillian, I've listened to all these things that your mother's told me, and I need to speak to her privately." He said, "Wait here. We'll be back; we won't be very long," and they went and left her.

But as they went out the room, he turned on the radio that was sitting on his desk. And when they got out the room, he said to her mother, "Just stand and watch her."

And the minute they left the room, she said, she was on her feet, moving to the music. And they watched for a few minutes and he turned to her mother and said, "Mrs. Lynne, Gillian isn't sick; she's a dancer. Take her to a dance school."

I said, "What happened?"

She said, "She did. I can't tell you how wonderful it was. We walked in this room and it was full of people like me. People who couldn't sit still. People who had to move to think…"

… Who had to *move* to *think*. They did ballet; they did tap; they did jazz; they did modern; they did contemporary. She was eventually auditioned for the Royal Ballet School; she became a soloist; she had a wonderful career at the Royal Ballet. She eventually graduated from the Royal Ballet School and founded her own company—the Gillian Lynne Dance Company—met Andrew

Lloyd Weber. She's been responsible for some of the most successful musical theater productions in history; she's given pleasure to millions; and she's a multi-millionaire.

Somebody else might have put her on medication and told her to calm down.

I didn't know who Gillian Lynne was at the time, but when squirmy little Cassie was three, I enrolled her in a classical ballet class, hoping it would help channel and focus some of her energy. For fifteen years she danced ballet, eventually on pointe. Watching her dance could move her father and me to tears. It didn't take long until that little wiggle worm had become a swan.

The one-size classroom does not fit all. But homeschool parents, who know their child the best, have the opportunity and the flexibility to customize their children's education to fit their own unique learning styles.

*As I considered homeschooling, and wondered if I was
qualified enough to teach my own kids, I realized who
the world's leading expert on them was— me.*

From wiggle
worm to
swan:
Cassie's ballet
journey,
beginning at
age three.

six

What About Socialization?

"I've seen the village, and I don't want it raising my kids."

— *Anonymous*

It was a delightful spring day for a picnic in the park. Cooper, who was almost three, and I met another mother and her son for a playdate near a playground. The boys naturally headed for the most dangerous thing there—a metal slide with a ladder that was at least ten-feet-high. Both boys started to climb the ladder. My friend and I got up off the bench to help them, when a young boy, about the age of ten or eleven, ran toward the slide.

"Don't worry! I'll help them!" he offered.

We watched as he gently helped our two-year-olds safely up the ladder and then applauded them as they reached the bottom of the slide. Around they went to do it again. Once again, the ten-year-old helped them up the ladder and down the slide. We watched this sweet kid play with our boys for about fifteen minutes, until he cheerfully waved to us.

"Gotta go!"

He ran towards a man just getting out of his car who was taking off his suit jacket and loosening his tie—obviously his dad taking a lunch break from work. They hugged and then joined the mom and his three younger brothers on a blanket. My friend and I were so impressed with this whole scene, especially the ten-year-old. Don't boys that age usually ignore younger kids?

We stopped by their picnic as we were leaving to thank the young man for helping our sons with the slide. The mother was beaming with pride.

"Are the schools out today?" I couldn't resist asking.

"Oh, we homeschool," she said smiling.

"Well, it's a great day to bring them to the park."

She touched her hand to her heart, "I love going anywhere with my boys."

I couldn't get over how calm and content she seemed when other mothers of four young boys might have been more frazzled or stressed. Something inside me knew I wanted what they had: time to enjoy a picnic in the park in the middle of the week, a close-knit family, considerate, polite kids, and what seemed to be a true enjoyment of one another's company. How much did their homeschooling have to do with all of this?

A few years later, a friend who was homeschooling invited me to visit her homeschool co-op so I could get an idea of what it offered. She and her husband had been working for years with a ministry to high school students called Young Life. We got out of her car together and were going through the parking lot towards the building when we walked near a couple of the co-op kids—a teenage girl and boy who were leaning against a car, talking. They stopped talking when they saw us approaching and the girl smiled.

"Can we help you find anything?" she asked.

"I've been here before but thank you so much for asking," my friend said.

Once we got inside she said, "Did you see that? Two homeschool teenagers stopped talking to each other, acknowledged us, and asked if we needed help. This doesn't happen when I visit teenagers at the regular schools."

So far, I had seen a homeschooled ten-year-old treat two-year-olds with kindness, and two homeschooled teenagers treat two adults with respect. I made a mental note to myself:

homeschooled kids seem comfortable interacting with people of all ages.

I wouldn't be surprised if you glanced at the Table of Contents and came to read this chapter first. "What about socialization?" is the question I'm asked most often when it comes to homeschooling. First, let's define what it means. Here is the primary definition the Merriam-Webster Dictionary gives for socialization: *the process beginning during childhood by which individuals acquire the values, habits, and attitudes of a society.*

When a young child is at home with a parent, that adult has the greatest impact on that child's socialization process. But once a child enters a classroom setting, where there is one adult to dozens of children, he will spend up to half of his waking hours mingling with, and taking social cues from, his peers. So, my question back to parents considering homeschooling is this: who do you want to teach your child the values, habits, and attitudes of our society? Other people's children? Or *you*?

People often equate the socialization of a child with the opportunity to interact with other children of their own age. I'm not sure how we got that idea. Another definition given for the word socialization is: *exposure of a young domestic animal (such as a kitten or puppy) to a variety of people, animals, and situations to minimize fear and aggression and promote friendliness.* Notice it says a *variety* of people, animals, and situations. When a dog owner takes their pet to a dog park to socialize with other animals, does it matter that the other dogs are all different ages, sizes, and breeds? Obviously not.

Merriam-Webster's final definition of socialization is: *social interaction with others.* Note that it doesn't say with others "of the same age." So why do schools group children by their age? Is it for the good of the child, or for the convenience of the teacher? It's true that it's not as easy to teach children of different ages all together, but that's exactly how it was done in the old one-room schoolhouses of our past. How in the world did a single teacher make that work?

My mother's father attended a one-room schoolhouse in rural East Texas. He and his siblings rode their horses to school and then the horses would walk back home. About a half hour before school ended, his mother would tell the horses, "Go get the kids." And the horses would walk back to the school and be there waiting for them when they got out. How fun is that?

Anyway, in this one-room schoolhouse his teacher would give the younger students an assignment to work on while she was teaching the older children. Then the teacher would enlist the older children to help her teach the younger ones, basically turning them into tutors.

Here's what is kind of genius about this arrangement: older kids usually respond really well to being given responsibility when they feel needed. They naturally enjoy playing a role in something larger than themselves. Remember the power of expectations? When the older children were expected to help teach the younger children, they rose to meet that high expectation. And what kid doesn't relish the opportunity to tell another kid something *they* know that the other kid doesn't?

It gets even better. In *The Seven Laws of the Teacher,* Dr. Howard Hendricks finds that people can generally remember about 10% of what they hear. If you add a visual, people can remember around 50% of what they hear and see. But if you add an activity, like teaching, you can remember up to 90% of what you hear, see, and do. So now you have the older kids teaching *and* remembering up to 90% of what they're teaching because it involves an activity.

And what about the "crowd control" in a one-room schoolhouse? Well, while the older students were on their best behavior because they were rising to the high expectations set for them, the younger kids, who love to mimic what older kids do, were copying the older kids, who were on their best behavior. As a result, everyone's behavior was (usually) elevated.

Contrast that with a room full of children the same age. It's fair to say they don't exactly bring out the best in one another. As peers, they are more likely to be one another's competitors, vying for attention, or for a spot in the social pecking order. And their behavior usually suffers from not being around better behaved older children; a single disruption, unplanned interruption, or the antics of a mischief-maker can send the entire class spiraling downward into chaos.

My grandfather, who grew up to become a surgeon, was extremely bright as a child. When he was one of the younger students, he tried to finish his assignments as fast as he could so he could listen in on what the older kids were learning. He was disappointed when he became one of the oldest students because he could no longer learn from the older students' lessons. When he got to the public high school, he must have been extra disappointed to find that a single-grade classroom can only move as fast as the slowest student.

Sadly, most of our one-room schoolhouses have been replaced. The closest thing I've experienced to one is a community college classroom due to the variety of ages and life stages. In a single class, you can have students ranging from young, recent high school graduates to much older people who are finally getting a degree or working toward a career change. I always enjoyed the discussions there because the older students asked such insightful questions. The diversity of ages and life experiences enriched us all.

If parents believe that one of the functions of a school is to socialize their children and to prepare them for life as an adult, then grouping them by their age seems like an odd way to do it. When else in their adult lives will that ever happen? Well, maybe when they enter a retirement community. But for the most part, a classroom of peers is a manufactured social construct they won't encounter again.

Wouldn't a more natural way to socialize children for their future adult life be to have the majority of their time spent around people of all ages? Spending a majority of their day with their peers leaves some kids very uncomfortable with people who are older or younger than themselves. When I would greet some of them at my church by looking them in the eye, smiling, and addressing them by name, I could get some very awkward responses—from little to no eye contact—or they just acted like I was invisible.

My children's homeschool experience included lots of time spent with their siblings, cousins, and grandparents. But they also had lots of opportunities to interact with their peers through dance lessons, sports, summer camps, co-op classes, and church. Homeschooling does not have to mean that your kids never see other kids their own age, it just means they won't spend most of their day with them.

Homeschoolers are sometimes unfairly stereotyped as being shy or awkward in social settings, and certainly, some of them are. But have you ever met a socially awkward student who attended public or private school? I have.

So how do homeschoolers, in general, compare socially to their classroom-educated peers? The National Home Education Research Institute conducted a study on the social, emotional, and psychological development of homeschooled kids. The research measures included: peer interaction, self-concept, leadership skills, family cohesion, participation in community service, and self-esteem. Their conclusion found homeschoolers to typically be "above average."

Anecdotally, I will say, after meeting hundreds of homeschoolers over the years, that as a group, they are some of the most impressive, polite people you will ever meet:

good eye contact, firm handshakes, attentive listeners, and excellent conversationalists. My son Cooper's homeschool basketball buddies are starting to get married and attending these weddings is a joy. Each of these boys, as the groom, has taken the time to greet us, address us by name, "Hello, Mr. and Mrs. Kelemen," ask about our daughters, and thank us for coming. They are simply delightful young men. They don't just seem like the kids of our friends, they feel like our friends too.

As I considered homeschooling, I asked myself, "Who do I want to have the most influence over my children's understanding of the values, habits, and attitudes of our society?" And I knew who I wanted that person to be—
me.

Goofing around with styrofoam teeth

seven

But What if My Kids Drive Me Crazy?

"Tell me and I'll forget, teach me and I'll remember, involve me and I'll learn."

– *Benjamin Franklin*

It was already getting dark as we were leaving our church. The kids and I had been to our Wednesday night activities, my husband was working late, and I was anxious to get them to bed so I could get some things done before I went to bed. But my son had just been given instructions for how to make "Mini S'mores."

"Can we make them, Mom, please?"

"Absolutely. We can make them tomorrow."

"Tonight, Mom! *Please*! Can we please make them tonight?"

I looked in the rearview mirror at three sets of pleading eyes and praying hands. They were still so little and cute, and they were begging to do something with their mom. How could I turn *that* down?

"Okay, why not?"

We stopped off at the grocery store and got the ingredients: Golden Grahams cereal, milk chocolate chips, and mini marshmallows. When we got home we all gathered around our breakfast table. I dimmed the light fixture for effect, and we leaned in to roast our marshmallows on toothpicks over a candle. As I looked around at their candlelit faces, I tried to make the moment stand still for just a second so I could take a mental snapshot. I have no recollection of what I thought was so important to get done that evening, but I'll never forget those little faces. And it reminded me of an important truth: in the long run, it's more important to do things *with* your kids than to do things *for* your kids.

The opportunity for parents to do things *with* their kids is the reason Walt Disney created his amusement parks.

"Disneyland really began," Walt once said, "when my two daughters were very young. Saturday was always Daddy's Day, and I would take them to the merry-go-round and sit on a bench eating peanuts while they rode. And sitting there, alone, I felt there should be something built, some kind of family park where parents and children could have fun *together*."

Of course, hanging out with your children at Disneyland sounds like fun. And I can understand why imagining yourself at home with your kids for much of the day might *not* sound like fun. But here's what I've found—the more time I spent with my kids, the more time I *wanted* to spend with my kids. As we discussed in the last chapter, one reason for this was our role in their socialization process. The homeschool lifestyle gave us the time we needed to help shape our children into the kind of people we wanted to be around.

Homeschooling also gave us the time to develop as a family. In general, the more time a family spends together, the stronger the relationships become, and the better the family members get along with each other.

I found a fascinating discussion on social media while the schools were closed during the pandemic lockdown. These school parents were astonished to discover that while their family was at home with one another almost all day, their children were actually getting along *better.* One dad said he used to have to constantly break up fights between his boys, ages nine and eleven, but during the lockdown, they started playing games with one another. They were very quiet one evening, so he cracked open their bedroom door and found them busy building an entire city out of Legos. One mom said she was amazed that the extra time spent with her unaffectionate six-year-old daughter had turned her into a super sweet cuddle bug—more hugs, kisses, and snuggling in her lap whenever she sat down.

Typically, the more time you spend with your kids, the more you will like and understand them, and the more they will like and understand you. Communication happens best within the context of a relationship, so the saying "People don't care how much you know until they know how much you care" is pretty accurate.

There's another saying, "It's not the *quantity* of time you spend with your kids that counts—it's the *quality*." I'm going to have to disagree with that. I have found that it's the quantity of time *that leads to* the quality of time. Those magical, teachable moments don't just happen. They can't be forced, they're organic. They appear suddenly, like a rainbow, out of an abundance of time spent together.

There's a wonderful book called *The Five Love Languages* by Gary Chapman. In it, you can take a little quiz to see how you best perceive love. The five ways are: words of affirmation, quality time, gifts, physical touch, and acts of service. For couples, it's important to tell your mates that you love them in the way they *perceive* it best, not in the way you *express* it best. However, all children have the same love language. It's spelled T-I-M-E. Spend *time* with me. When you spend your time with your children, you are communicating that you love them in the love language *they* understand best.

Every fall, the kids and I would take a field trip to the state fair on opening day. We all had our favorite foods and events that we wanted to experience every time we went. One year, opening day fell on Cooper's tenth birthday. Russ hugged us goodbye and told us to have a wonderful day at the fair and then drove off to work. Little did Cooper know, he was just dropping off some things for the substitute teacher. When he returned a short while later, Cooper was shocked.

"What are you doing home?"

"I've taken the day off—I'm going to the fair with you!"

Cooper ran to hug his dad as all of our eyes were tearing up. For him, that gift of time said

"I love you" better than any other birthday present could have.

It's unfortunate that most school schedules get in the way of families spending crucial time together. As a result, many parents only have enough time to do things for their kids instead of with them. They drive, clean, wash, and cook for their kids, understandably, because their kids have been out of the house all day. But when the greater part of a parent's time with their children is spent *serving* them, it's tempting for the children to see them as a servant.

I'm glad my kids were around to see what happened in our home all day and what it took to make it function. While they were doing a lesson at the breakfast table, my kids would see me doing things like load the dishwasher, pay some bills, or put a stew in the slow cooker. As they grew older, they helped more with the chores as they were able. But taking care of our household was something we all did together.

Of course, I served my kids too, but I'm grateful I had the time to make my role in their lives much bigger than that. The mom my kids saw mop the floor was the same mom who taught them how to read, helped them with their math, and practiced recognizing logical fallacies with them. As a result, they didn't just see me as their driver, or their laundress, or their maid, or their cook. I was their mom, but I was also their teacher. That earned their respect. And—most of the time—kids who respect you don't drive you crazy.

As I considered homeschooling, I wanted my kids' schedule to have the room to include doing things with—me.

Hanging out at the Grand Canyon

eight

Will I Have Time to Homeschool?

"Children are not a distraction from the more important work—they are the most important work."

– C. S. Lewis

During the 1976 Montreal Summer Olympic Games, Nadia Comaneci, a 14-year-old Romanian gymnast, became a legend. During the team competition, she performed a routine on the uneven bars flawlessly, stuck the landing, and then waited for her score. The crowd was shocked when the score board read 1.00. Everyone was confused, especially Nadia. Finally, since a 10.00 had never been awarded before, it was announced that because the scoreboard could only go up to 9.95, the judges had to enter 1.00 to convey she had received a perfect score! She went on to win the gold medal in the individual all-around and received a total of seven perfect 10s.

As a small kid watching all of this, I wondered how Nadia had the time to become that good at gymnastics. I thought about my own life: school most of the day, after-school lessons, homework, chores, dinner, a little playtime with neighborhood friends, and then bedtime. How did Nadia fit the training it took to become a world-class gymnast into her schedule?

Then I found out that Nadia didn't go to regular school like I did. Similar to Gillian Lynne's mother, Nadia's mother found her so active, energetic, and difficult to manage that she enrolled her in a gymnastics school. A video about her training revealed she spent around 6 hours a day working in the gym and a couple of hours a day with a tutor on school subjects.

A couple of hours! She got all of her school done in a couple of hours? How come my school takes so much longer?

But when I thought about my typical school day, it included a lot of extras like announcements, lunch, and recess. One public school educator tallied how many hours it would take to teach someone all of the foundational math, reading, and writing that are essential to know as an adult, and it came to around 100 hours. Compare that with how many hours a student spends at a traditional K–12 school, and it comes to around 25,000 hours!

While I was researching homeschooling, the first book I read about it was written by a Californian mother with seven kids. She lamented that it took way too much of her day to get all of her children ready for school, get them to school, get them back from school, and then try to figure out what they were supposed to do for homework before they went back to school the next day. And the homework load was beyond ridiculous.

"What in the world are you doing there all day?" she would ask her kids.

Then one day, as she was rummaging through her son's backpack looking for his assignment instructions, and then trying to decipher what had been covered in class and what was homework, she became increasingly frustrated.

"I bet it would take less time to just school them myself," she muttered.

Light bulb moment! Not long after, she began homeschooling and discovered she was right.

One of my favorite things about homeschooling is how incredibly efficient it is. When someone tells me they'd never have enough time to homeschool, they're probably trying to imagine themselves recreating a typical school day in a traditional classroom at home. I love the looks people give me when I tell them I probably spend *less* time schooling my own kids than they spend transporting theirs to and from school and then trying to get them to finish their homework.

So how long does it take? The time requirements change depending on the age of your children, but as my role evolved from teacher, to tutor, to monitor, our homeschool days required no more than around two to four hours a day of my direct involvement. That's it.

There are many ways to do it, but I generally structured our day into two parts. We did the "table work" first, like math, science, spelling, and writing assignments. Then we had what I called "story time" when I read aloud the history and literature that our curriculum coordinated around a place or period in time. As the kids got older, they worked and read more and more on their own. Depending on when we got started in the morning, many days we could be finished before lunch or at least by early afternoon. And this opened up an enormous amount of free time that we could use in other ways.

For example, that extra time changed the way we spent our evenings together. As someone who is married to a public school teacher, the last thing I wanted Russ to see when he came home from work was his own kids doing school. It was a great pleasure to have them completely done for the day and there was no need for him to be the homework police. Whenever we were out of the house and he beat us home, as soon as I lifted the garage door and they could see his car was there, they'd start a "Daddy's home! Daddy's home!" chant and run in to greet him. I loved that he was free to spend his evenings just playing with the kids or hanging out as a family.

The extra time also gave our kids lots of private time and space—quiet time, down time —just to be a child, to piddle, to play, to develop their own identity, and to dream. How are children supposed to grow up and work to achieve their dreams if they never have the time to dream in the first place? How can they ever march to the beat of their own drummer if their environment is too noisy to hear the drum?

Even though my kids' "screen time" with electronics was very limited, I rarely heard "I'm bored" or "There's nothing to do" from any of them. They enthusiastically embraced free time and were very comfortable with being unscheduled. But I know ultra-scheduled kids whose parents feel like they have to keep them "entertained" during school holidays. It's exhausting. And regrettably, these parents are relieved when their kids go back to school.

My kids also had the time to follow their interests. I remember in ninth grade coming to a unit on Greek mythology. I loved it! I was fascinated by how the Greeks used stories to explain things in nature they didn't fully understand, like why the seasons changed, or how the Milky Way got its place in the sky. I wanted to know more about it—all about it—but according to the teacher's schedule, it was time to move on. I was so disappointed.

There's a demotivating effect on students who are not often afforded the chance to follow what interests them. After John Taylor Gatto retired from teaching public school in New York City for thirty years, he made a similar observation in his book *Dumbing Us Down*. For years, he watched students who were right in the middle of something that sparked their interest. And then the bell rang. Time to change classes. Over time, the unspoken message to the student is that the school schedule is more important than what they are doing at that moment. It's understandable when some of them conclude that since the schedule is most important, then maybe what they're working on isn't worth caring about; or worse, if finishing something isn't important, why start it in the first place?

Of course, an institutionalized school with its hundreds of students would be in complete chaos and couldn't possibly function without schedules and bells. But that's my point. When the student is removed from the institution, the parent and child have the freedom to mold the schedule around the student, instead of the other way around.

After I taught my oldest how to read, I was disappointed that he just wasn't that interested in doing it. But one day he read a children's book about Robinson Caruso, and he was hooked—the flame was ignited! Then one of his friends mentioned *The Hardy Boys* books. Once he read one, the race was on! He decided he wanted to read them all. Every time we drove past a library, we would stop and go in to see if there was one on their shelves he hadn't read yet. He started keeping a list and even timed himself on how long it took him to read one cover to cover. He got it down to an hour and a half! Did I care that we weren't exactly following our curriculum at the moment? Not at all. What Cooper was doing at that point in time was way more important—he was reading for the sheer pleasure of it and learning to love it. Why would I want to interrupt *that*?

As the youngest child in my family, I often felt a bit rushed. Because my parents were trying to keep up with my older siblings, I didn't always get to move at my desired pace, which was along the lines of a distracted turtle. I really didn't like being hurried, and I wanted to avoid hurrying my own kids if I could. The homeschool lifestyle didn't just slow life down for my kids, it slowed it down for *me*. One morning, as I heard the carpool horns honking on my street, I looked over at my kids, eating cereal in their pajamas, knowing we would soon be snuggled on the sofa together engrossed in a good book, and I inhaled deeply and smiled.

This unhurried lifestyle also gave my kids the time to follow their curiosity. One morning, as we were eating breakfast, I poured some milk and set the plastic jug down on the table but didn't push the top all the way down. A good minute later, POP! the top came off and landed on the table. We all looked at each other with wide eyes. Catie shouted, "Why did it do that?" Cassie wanted to see if it would do it again, so she lightly set the top back on the jug, and sure enough, it lifted and came back down like a little burp. Cooper ran to the family computer to see if he could find out what happened. A few minutes later he proclaimed, "Hot air rises!"

We figured out together that because the jug was half-full of cold milk and half-full of cold air that when I poured some milk out, some of the cold air came out too and was replaced by warmer air. That warm air rose to the top and pushed the lid off. There. A mini science lesson before we finished breakfast.

Lastly, all that extra time gave my kids the chance to hone in on some specific skills. It's great to introduce kids to a variety of things, but they also need the option to focus in on a few select things, or they risk becoming flat. If Nadia Comaneci was only a little bit good at a lot of things, we probably would have never heard of her. But instead, she was able to focus on, and excel, at just one thing. And why not? Is it really the jacks-of-all-trades who leave a mark on this world, or is it those who are the master of one?

Cassie inherited her grandmother's musical ear. Our house was too small for a piano, so I got her a child-sized violin and lessons from a neighbor. When we were finally able to get a piano, she couldn't keep her hands off of it. Every free moment she had led her to that piano, and she filled our house with music.

As an early teen, she was able to master "Claire de Lune" by Claude Debussy. We invited one of our neighbors, Mary, over for dinner one night. Mary's cancer treatments were failing, and she didn't have much time left. After we ate, we had Cassie play the piano for her. I watched Mary lift her chin, close her eyes, and try to absorb every note until a tear started rolling down her cheek. There's a compassion that emanates from Cassie's interpretation of music, and Mary felt it. Cassie also sings, plays the guitar, ukulele, and mandolin—all self-taught. There are lots of kids with lots of God-given talent, and I'm glad I could give my kids the time to develop theirs.

While I was taking a creative writing class in my twenties, I learned that children do not have to be taught how to be creative, *adults* do. Somewhere between our childhood and our adulthood, the creative right side of our brain gets put on the back burner while we are educated in left-brain-leaning classrooms. I vowed to myself way back then that I would do the best I could to preserve the natural creativity of my future children.

That vow paid off in spades with Catie, who is a visual learner with an eye for design. She took dance, music and horseback riding lessons, but she particularly excels at anything visual, like photography, arranging flowers, and decorating spectacular cakes. It wasn't until she took an elective class in painting at a community college that we understood what an artist she is. Her first assignment was a black and white still life of three household objects. I think she nailed it—it's hard to tell it's not a black and white photograph! Since then, she has filled our home with some wonderful paintings. What a delight to drive up to our house and see her painting a canvas on our front porch.

Early on, Cooper showed interest in the arts. Before he was twelve, he won two art contests, placed in the state fair cookie decorating contest, and won several lead roles in church musicals. He's also an accomplished self-taught guitarist and gifted athlete. As a teenager, he would use a lot of his spare time shooting basketball hoops. Study a little, shoot hoops. Study a little more, shoot hoops. Over time, he developed a pretty reliable three-point shot. One evening, his homeschool basketball team was playing a private school and Cooper just couldn't miss that day—he made seven beautifully arched, net-swishing three-point shots. One of the private school fathers came to find us after the game.

"How did your son get that lethal three-point shot?" he asked.

"Well," I said, "because we homeschool, he has lots of free time to practice."

As I considered homeschooling, I knew I wanted a slower pace, a calmer lifestyle, and plenty of unhurried, unscheduled free time—not just for my kids but for— me.

Catie's first painting, Catie's dance recital, Cassie's piano recital, Cooper's basketball tournament

nine

What if My Kids Get Bored?

"Educating the mind without educating the heart is no education at all."

— *Aristotle*

In the fifth grade, I was told I had to memorize a list of nineteen simple qualifier pronouns for a quiz the next day. My grade would be determined by how many I could remember and write down. I had memorized many things before, but this assignment stumped me; it was just a list of words that didn't seem to have anything to do with one another. I was learning to play the ukulele at the time, and my dad had taught me how to play "Five Foot Two, Eyes of Blue." So, I set the list of pronouns to that tune and sang it several times that night and a few times before school. Not only did I remember all nineteen pronouns for the quiz, but to this day, decades later, I can still sing that song.

Most of us were asked to memorize things during our school days. Some things were memorized due to repetition, like the Pledge of Allegiance, but other methods, like flashcards, were used to memorize things like the multiplication table. Even as we got older, we were still memorizing or more like "cramming" information into our heads, so we could spit it out for a test and then promptly forget it. It wasn't fun at all; it was exasperating.

I remember wondering, *What's the point?*

Have you ever heard an old song that you haven't heard in years, and somehow you remember every single syllable of the lyrics, down to the ad libs of the singer? There's something magical about the connection between words and music that burns itself into our memories with little effort. So why isn't music used to help students memorize more often?

One example of educational music is "School House Rock," the animated short films that first appeared during Saturday morning cartoons in the 1970s. It used songs to teach things like history, civics, and grammar. I loved those songs as a kid, and I wanted to use music as much as I could with my own kids. That's why I was excited to find a math curriculum that uses "skip counting" songs to teach the multiplication table. For example, multiplication by threes is set to the tune of "Jingle Bells."

Three, six, nine, twelve, fifteen, eighteen, twenty-one,

Twenty-four, and twenty-seven, isn't counting fun?

Three, six, nine, twelve, fifteen, eighteen, twenty-one,

Twenty-four, and twenty-seven, thirty, and we're done!

It only took my kids a few days before they had learned all twelve skip counting songs. They could figure out any multiplication equation by silently singing it to themselves. Eventually, they didn't need to recall the song anymore—it had been downloaded to their mental hard drive. No flashcards, no pain, and so much more fun. We found other music curriculums to help us memorize all kinds of things: the US presidents, world geography, grammar rules, and even the animal kingdom for biology. And like me, years later, my kids can still sing these songs!

I had solved the memorization bane of my educational experience for my kids with music, but there was another nuisance I had to do something about—textbooks. I found them uninteresting; they weighed down my backpack, and I honestly can't recall much about a single one of them.

So what do I remember when I look back on my school years? Easy. The stories—the after-lunch storybooks read aloud by my teachers in elementary school, the Greek mythology unit in junior high, the classical book assignments in high school English, and the gifted storytelling history professor in college.

Stories are the single most effective communication tool for several reasons. First, they have an extraordinary ability to stay with you. Nothing can have a lasting impact on you if you can't remember it. But stories create a picture, or mental image, in your mind's eye. That means when you hear a story, you're not just hearing it, you're effectively seeing it too. And remember, you only recall about 10% of what you *hear*, but up to 50% of what you *hear* and *see*. You can tell a child, "Always tell the truth or people will stop believing you," or you can tell him the story about "The Boy Who Cried 'Wolf.'" Which one will he most likely remember?

Next, stories have the unique capacity for breaking through our paradigms, or working models. These are the pictures in our mind that we use to make sense of how something works, like how the picture on a puzzle's box top makes sense of the puzzle pieces inside. We develop working models for all kinds of different things without even being aware of it, mostly from our personal experiences. For example, when you think about a card game you know how to play, did you learn it by reading the instructions, or just by playing a few rounds until you caught on?

It's surprising how loyal we are to our models. They are a lot like Mary Flo's curiosity sponges—once they're formed, conflicting data will just kind of roll off. That's why they can be an obstacle when it comes to getting someone to contemplate something new or different from what they have personally experienced.

But there is a way around it. Since we don't have time to create working models for everything based on our *own* personal experiences, we often rely on the personal experiences of *others*. Stories, eyewitness accounts, anecdotes, testimonies, fables, and parables, if well-told, can replace an old mental image with a brand new picture in the mind of the listener.

Stories can get past mental obstacles and defenses like nothing else can. For instance, an ancient story about King David illustrates how powerful a story can be. Long ago, while his men were at war, David stayed home, saw Bathsheba, and had her husband killed so he could have her for himself.

So, God sent the prophet Nathan to tell him this story:

There were two men in a certain city, one very rich, owning many flocks of sheep and herds of goats; the other very poor, owning nothing but a little lamb he had managed to buy. It was his children's pet, and he fed it from his own plate and let it drink from his own cup; he cuddled it in his arms like a baby daughter. Recently, a guest arrived at the home of the rich man. But instead of killing a lamb from his own flocks for food for the traveler, he took the poor man's lamb and roasted it and served it."

David was furious.

"I swear by the living God," he vowed, "any man who would do a thing like that should be put to death; he shall repay four lambs to the poor man for the one he stole and for having no pity."

> Then Nathan said to David, "You are that rich man!" 2 Samuel 11-12

Oof. This story slipped right through David's mental and emotional defenses and went straight to his heart. Not only did that story lead to David's immediate contrition, but it likely kept Nathan from being killed on the spot for having dared to confront the king.

Finally, stories are effective because they're interesting. Books that tell stories have characters you care about, a setting you can visualize, a dramatic plot that pulls you in, exciting conflicts, meaningful resolutions, and a lesson to be learned. Stories that have these elements, and that are written by a single author, are what English educator, Charlotte Mason (1842-1923), called a "whole book" or a "living book." During her day, the living books that had been the staple of education were replaced by textbooks—books that were written by a committee of people with dry facts and disjointed information. She called them "twaddle."

When I started my search for curriculums, I was delighted to find so many of them that are Charlotte Mason-inspired. Of course, textbooks on some subjects cannot be avoided, but a literature-based curriculum will use a living book whenever possible. We especially enjoyed the biographies and historical-based fiction because the settings were so vivid. They transported us to a time and place in history and made us see real events through the eyes of a relatable character.

The hours I spent with my kids reading wonderful books together became a shared experience between us that knit us together as a family. When we were traveling in London and Paris, the kids would bring up memories and scenes from our books that had taken place there; it was almost like we had been there together before.

As the kids got older, some of the assigned classical literature had more difficult language, but I didn't want that getting in the way of the marvelous storylines. When it came to read one of my favorites, *Tale of Two Cities* by Charles Dickens, I found a version with the original text side by side with a modern translation. I would go back and forth between the two, depending on the difficulty of the passage. But I loved it when I would read from the modern version to hear the kids ask, "How did Dickens say it?"

They were all teenagers when we got to Jane Austen's *Pride and Prejudice*. I had to reassess my goal—was it just to get through the book? No. I wanted them to *love* it. So I compromised and found a chapter by chapter, faithful-to-the-text BBC production of the book. While my daughters were wooed by Mr. Darcy, my son was more interested in learning *how* to woo like Mr. Darcy. And despite viewing it from their different angles, my goal was accomplished—they all ended up loving it.

Since stories were the favorite part of my education, I happily used them whenever I could. It's true that most things are *caught* rather than *taught*, and a child can't help but catch the contagious enthusiasm of an author telling their own story about the meaningful things in life.

We don't read and write poetry because it's cute. We read and write poetry because we are members of the human race. And the human race is filled with passion. And medicine, law, business, engineering, these are noble pursuits and necessary to sustain life. But poetry, beauty, romance, love, these are what we stay alive for.

– from the movie "Dead Poet's Society"

As I considered homeschooling, I knew things like stories and music could make my kids' education more fun, and I knew who would be thrilled to use them— me.

Celebrating the Pacific Ocean on the coast of Oregon

ten

What if I Leave Out Something They Should Know?

"Education is the kindling of a flame, not the filling of a vessel."

— *Socrates*

While studying in London during college I was able to visit Westminster Abbey. And because I was taking English and history classes at the time, I was impressed with the people I recognized who were buried there—people like Henry V, Elizabeth I, Mary Queen of Scots, Charles Dickens, Robert Browning, Geoffrey Chaucer, John Milton, and Isaac Newton.

Years later, one of the books that came with our homeschool curriculum was about William Wilberforce (1759-1833). I wasn't familiar with him. In fact, I don't recall having ever heard of him. It was a short, simple child's biography, but I was absolutely floored when I learned about what this man had accomplished.

As a member of the British Parliament, Wilberforce was convinced by an anti-slave-trade activist named Thomas Clarkson to champion the abolitionist movement. For twenty years, he spearheaded the parliamentary campaign against the British slave trade until the Slave Trade Act of 1807 was passed. He continued the fight by supporting the campaign for the Slavery Abolition Act of 1833, which ended slavery in most of the British Empire. Wilberforce died three days after its passage. Parliament closed down out of respect while many of its members joined a procession of his casket to Westminster Abbey where he was buried.

One persistent man, a member of parliament, who spent decades escorting a cause through a maze of obstacles and opponents, who finally, without bloodshed, succeeded at what took America 500,000 lives to accomplish—the end of slavery in the British Empire! How had I never heard of him before? How did William Wilberforce slip through the cracks in my education? Why did it take homeschooling my own children before I found out about this monumentally consequential man?

The next time I went to Westminster Abbey, it was with my husband and kids. This time, I didn't care as much about monarchs or poets or scientists. The kids and I knew exactly who we wanted to find first. The stone walls and floors of the abbey magnified every sound, so we whispered as we wandered past monument after marker until there, in the North Choir Aisle, we finally found him—a statue of William

Wilberforce. Even though we tried to muffle our reaction, our enthusiasm turned the heads of nearby guests as they wondered whom we had discovered. I remember standing there, in awed admiration and overwhelming gratitude for his life. And to think, I probably strolled right past that statue when I was a college student. What a difference there was between my two trips to Westminster Abbey, and it was all because of the history I knew.

History—what a loaded subject, especially now. Do our classrooms revise it or teach it unrevised? What has been left in? What has been left out? And who decides? The good news is, if you choose to homeschool your children, *you* get to decide.

What goes in and what stays out of a child's education in a traditional school is an interesting process. Somehow a group of somebodies agrees on a body of knowledge that every student should know. Then they divide it up by subject and grade, spread it out over twelve years, and call it a "scope and sequence." The child is then "filled" with this body of knowledge, little by little, until he's deemed "full" and handed a diploma.

Socrates was right. True education is more like the lighting of a fire. It takes a child's natural love of learning, his spark of curiosity, and ignites it into a flame, then fans it into a fire that will burn for a lifetime. The goal of education shouldn't be to teach a student everything he "should know" because "what should be known" is subjective, and not every student is alike. No, the goal of education should be to create self-learners—people who continue to follow their interests and curiosity throughout their lives and learn how to learn about what they want to know.

Whoever decided to call a graduation ceremony a "commencement" understood this. Commencement literally means "beginning." In other words, this ceremony marks the end of your formal education and the beginning of your lifelong self-education.

Some parents I've spoken with are intimidated by the impression that they have to be a bottomless well of knowledge in order to homeschool. A few of them have asked me

"What if my child asks me a question, and I don't know the answer?" I tell them, "Fantastic! Praise your kid for asking such a great question and then find out the answer together. Show your child what adults do when they come across something they don't know—they figure out how to find out about it."

When the kids were young, I read them a book about an Italian village on the island of Capri that had a mysterious, haunted cave called The Blue Grotto. Many sailors went in who never came out. For generations, people were too afraid to enter the cave, until someone was finally brave enough to figure out what was happening. Past sailors had entered the cave at low tide, but once inside they became disoriented because the walls and ceiling of the cave were the same bright blue as the water. Unable to navigate their way out in time, the tide would rise, and they would drown.

After we finished the book, one of them asked, "Mom, is this a real place, or is it just in the book?"

"You know, I don't know," I answered. I really didn't. So, we all went over to the family computer and searched "Blue Grotto, Capri." Up came the most gorgeous images of this spectacular cave, so completely washed in glowing turquoise on the inside that the boats appeared to be floating in mid-air. The kids started jumping up and down with excitement.

"It's real! It's real! It's real!"

We had all learned something new together, at the same time, and it was exhilarating!

As I considered homeschooling, I knew I couldn't teach my kids everything, but I also knew who I wanted to decide what was important for them to know—— me.

The Kelemen family in front of Westminster Abbey

eleven

How Do You Grade Your Own Kid?

"I have never let my schooling interfere with my education."

– Mark Twain

It was finals week during my first semester of my freshmen year in college. I was taking Intro to Psychology in a huge lecture hall of around two hundred students. Due to the size of the class, all of our tests were multiple choice—the kind where you filled in the bubbles on a strip for scanning. Before the first test, our professor said, "Remember class, there can be more than one right answer, but one of them is more right than the others."

Oh, great. This is not good, I thought.

I am one of those people who can make the case for multiple points of view at the same time. As I read through the test, I wasn't just trying to *remember* psychology, I was trying to *perform* psychology on my professor. I knew which answer *I* thought was right, but which answer did *he* think was right? I was probably overthinking, and it didn't go well. My test grades were pitiful.

Before the final, I went to see him in his office and explained my dilemma.

"I just don't think the tests are reflecting what I've learned. Is there any way I can do better in your class?"

He looked at his grade book, took out his calculator, averaged out my grades and said,

"Yep. If you make a one hundred on the final, you can just squeak out an A in my class."

Was he kidding? A one hundred? I just looked at him and blinked. "How would you suggest I do that?" It was an honest question.

And then he told me what he told the rest of the class: during finals week his office would be open, and we would be able to look over the answer keys to all of the prior tests.

So, the day before the final, I took him up on his offer and went to his office. There was a small waiting room with a coffee table in the middle, and on that table were the answer keys to the prior tests—about eight to ten of them, with fifty questions on each. I picked up test number one, read the first few questions and then tried to figure out why the correct answer was correct. Then I realized that this method was going to take forever. So I read the question, and the correct answer only. I read through each test twice, reading the question, and only the correct answer. It took me a couple of hours, and while I was there only a few other students came in to look over the tests.

The next day was the final. It was the last day of exams, and the campus was almost empty—most everyone else had already left town for the holidays. I walked into the lecture hall with my No. 2 pencils in hand. A couple of students helped pass out the stack of tests to the class. It was thick—at least a hundred questions. We had two hours to complete it. I took a deep breath and read question one. Gosh, it sounded familiar.

I think I read this same question yesterday.

I looked at the four possible answers, and one of them jumped out at me like it had been highlighted. So I bubbled it in. Next question— same as before.

*I **know** I read this question yesterday.* And again, only one of the answers looked familiar. *This must be it.*

So I bubbled it in. As I went down the page, every single question on the final had been taken from one of the prior tests—the exact same question with the exact same set of possible answers. And because I had only read the correct answer, they were easy to spot because they were the only ones that sounded familiar. I finished the exam and looked at the clock—it had only been fifteen minutes. So, I carefully looked over each question and answer again. Yes, I was satisfied that I had them all correct. I stood up to go lay the exam on the teacher's desk, and I heard some gasps and murmurs.

*What? She's **done**?*

I felt kind of sheepish as I walked out of that lecture hall, like I had cheated or done something wrong. But I hadn't.

A couple of weeks later, while I was out-of-town, my parents called to tell me my grades had come in the mail.

"Do you want us to open it?"

"Yes! Just tell me what I made in psychology."

"You made an A."

I couldn't believe it. I had made a one hundred on the final exam! And even though I was mentally celebrating, something in the back of my mind knew that what I really learned wasn't psychology—it was how to play the system. Because the class was so large, the professor was stuck with a testing and grading system that didn't, and couldn't, really measure what we knew. Oh well. On the bright side, there is one lesson I learned from this that has stayed with me all these years: *It pays to ask.*

What really is the purpose of grading and testing? Generally speaking, it is done so that a teacher with many students can keep track of their progress. Are they getting their assignments done? Are they learning the material? In other words, it's done for the sake of the teacher and not the student.

"Is this going to be on the test?" is a common question in many classrooms. For some students, tests have become a hoop to jump through, and they learn, like I did, how to play the system instead of truly learning the subject. And for some teachers, standardized tests have become *their* hoop to jump through. If their students do well on the standardized test, then they will get a good grade as a teacher. And so "what's on the test" becomes the main or even sole focus of their teaching.

Fortunately, parents that homeschool have a much easier time assessing what their kids know. When classroom students read a book, they usually have to write a book report to "prove" it. But isn't that like punishing a child for reading a book? Besides not being fun, a book report can cause their left brain, which puts "parts" before the "whole," to take over when they begin to write, and they can miss the big picture of the story by getting overwhelmed with the details.

But there's a better way to find out what your children have gleaned from a book they have either read or heard: switch roles and let *them* teach *you* about the book. Charlotte Mason calls this "narration." No paper, no pens, just let them tell you about the story in the book. This allows their right brain, which sees the "whole" before the "parts," to go first. A very general prompt, like "Tell me about the book you just read" starts a process in the child's mind. They have to develop a train of thought, prioritize which parts of the story are important to include, and put the events in their proper sequence. As they retell the story, they are internalizing it by adding some of their own observations and including their own personality. And they are learning how to think right before your eyes.

Another way to "grade" homeschoolers is to allow them to take a part in it. When my kids were small and practicing their handwriting, I would write a letter, like "m" at the top of the page and then show them how to make one. Then I would watch them make a row of "m's" and ask, "Which 'm' do you think is your very best?"

Then I would ask them, "Can you write another row and make them look just like your best one?"

Now instead of copying my "m," they were copying their own, and in the process, taking pride in their own work.

Homeschool grading also offers some special advantages when it comes to correcting mistakes. I remember as a child taking a test, and then a day or more later having it handed back to me with big red Xs next to what I had gotten wrong. The time gap from when I took the test, to when I received it back, had given just as much time for my wrong answers to sink into my mind as my right answers. Days later, that often led to confusion as I struggled to remember and understand where I had gone wrong. But when you're personally tutoring your child, you can quickly correct mistakes on the spot before they have time to sink in and while everything is fresh in your child's mind.

Some children are especially hard on themselves when they make mistakes. If you have one of these, perhaps for this child, you put checkmarks next to what she gets right instead of Xs next to what she gets wrong. You can also help to make mistakes more easily forgivable. For example, instead of writing on a paper tablet that makes erasing difficult and leaves an imprint on the pages below, give her a small dry erase board. For beginning writers, the marker has way less friction than pencil on paper and mistakes are gone with the just the swipe of a finger!

As I considered homeschooling, I knew the person who could most easily tell what my kids knew without tests and book reports would be— me.

Photographer dad finally makes it into a photo

twelve

Won't My Kids Feel Like They're Missing Out?

"I learned most, not from those who taught me but from those who talked with me."

— Saint Augustine

There was a deep cavern in a state park that was a popular destination for school field trips. The guide was used to giving large school groups guided tours into the cave, but one day a homeschool group organized enough families for a tour of their own. There were a variety of ages in the group, from four and five-year-olds to teenagers, with some of them carrying a toddler sibling on their hip or back.

Though she didn't know what to expect at first, the guide ended up being very impressed with this group of kids: they listened intently, asked insightful questions, addressed her politely, and were very respectful and well-behaved. At the end, they individually thanked her for the tour. The only thing the homeschoolers didn't do, she said later, was line up when she asked them to. When she said, "Line up!" they looked at her, and then as a group, they all just kind of scooted in closer.

So, if you choose to homeschool your kids, they will miss out on knowing how to line up. Bummer.

Homeschoolers will also miss out on homework. *All* of a homeschool kid's work is homework, but they can complete their work a lot quicker than a school schedule would allow. One spring, I could see that we had a very busy May ahead of us—music recitals, dance recitals, choir programs, and just a lot of year-end things. I asked the kids if they would like to finish school early, but we would have to "double up" the whole month of April. They were up for it! So, we worked extra hard and finished our school year by the first of May. We were all very proud of ourselves and had a great sense of accomplishment.

That May, the two weeks before Cassie and Catie's dance recital, was full of extra Saturday rehearsals, a run through, and a dress rehearsal in a university auditorium that always ran late. Most of their friends would bring their backpacks into the dressing room so they could get some of their homework assignments done while they were waiting to go on stage. One of them noticed Cassie didn't have a backpack full of books with her.

"Where are your schoolbooks? Don't you have homework?"

"No. I'm all done. We already finished school for the year."

"Lucky! I wish I was homeschooled!"

My kids often got comments like these from their friends who attended traditional schools, and that made them feel like *they* were not the ones who were missing out!

But homeschoolers will miss out on high school reunions. You know, those events where you gather every few years to see how well, or how poorly, your former classmates are aging. Even though people who attend large schools meet lots of people their own age, in the end, they usually keep up with very few of them on an on-going basis. As students grow up, get jobs and start families, their friendships often change to reflect their stage in life, and that's very typical.

I met one of my dear friends after college at a MOPS (Mothers of Preschoolers) meeting. Our infant sons were just a month apart in age. Then our second children, our daughters, were only a few days apart. Our whole families have remained friends all these years. Their son, Jack, played sports and had lots of friends from his large public high school. He attended an out-of-state university, and his mom would hold a get-together for him when he came home so he could easily see all his old high school classmates and friends. As the semesters went by, the circle of friends he wished to keep up with grew smaller and smaller. The last time his mom asked him, "Who do you want to see?"

He said, "Just Cooper."

A few years later when Jack got married, out of all of those friends from high school, he picked his homeschool buddy from church to be his best man.

As homeschooling has grown in popularity, there are fewer and fewer things that homeschoolers will miss by not being in a traditional school. When I first started homeschooling my kids, it was rare to see a child older than five out in public during school hours. In the beginning, if we were out in public, we got some strange looks and even some questions. But even in a few short years, homeschooling was becoming so much more common that no one said a word or even noticed us when we were out during the day. Because the number of homeschool families is growing, they are organizing more and offering a lot to the homeschool community. Here are a few examples:

Organized Sports

Where we live there are many homeschool sports teams that offer all of the sports, including cheerleading, for both girls and boys. They compete against one another, but also play some private schools and public schools too. In our state, my son's basketball organization had regional, state, and national tournaments that, at the time, included 309 teams from 38 states. Each season concluded with a sports banquet and awards ceremony for the athletes and their parents.

Co-ops and Dual-credit Classes

Co-ops are groups of homeschoolers that offer group field trips, extracurricular activities, support for parents, and even classes taught by parents, most of whom are wonderful empty-nest homeschoolers. One of many co-ops in my area offers almost any class you can think of, ranging from basics like math, science, English, and foreign languages, to electives like music, band, photography, robotics, and sign language.

They also offer things like achievement testing, college prep boot camp, spring break trips, and community service projects. And it is very affordable.

Dual-credit classes for junior and senior year high school students are available at the community colleges in my county for free, if you live in the county and are eighteen years of age or younger. This allows a student to get both high school and college credit at the same time for the same course. I found dual-credit classes to be better than advanced placement classes because there is no AP test at the end; the student achieves the credit for simply passing the class. The credits transferred to Cooper and Cassie's university as "passed" and did not affect their grade point average.

I also thought they were a great way for my kids to get some classroom experience before they went to college. But best of all, it saved a ton of money! Cooper went to college with 27 college hours under his belt, and he was able to graduate early even while gaining job experience by working for the university. Cassie had 36 hours and was able to complete her college degree in five semesters at age twenty. Catie continued on at her community college and completed her first two years (Associate degree) for only the price of books. That gave her what she needed to then pursue a certification in a specialized field. Check out the community colleges in your area to see if they offer a dual-credit program.

Homeschool Prom and Graduation Ceremonies

It took over 1,600 volunteers to pull off the homeschool prom in my city. I've never seen anything like it: motifs worthy of a movie set, theme-coordinated decorations, a seated dinner in a spectacular ballroom, a dance floor, tasteful music, and 2,000 homeschoolers having a night they'll always remember. Some co-ops also offer graduation ceremonies, complete with diplomas, cap and gowns, and include meaningful tributes from the parents.

As I considered homeschooling, the last person who wanted my kids to miss out on anything truly important was— me.

Cooper and Jack: from best buddies to best man

thirteen

What About Getting into College or Getting a Job?

"All men who have turned out worth anything have had the chief hand in their own education."

— *Walter Scott*

A college professor who taught freshmen science at a large midwest university liked to do a little experiment with his students. Every year he would give them written questions to answer on topics he covered in class, and then out of curiosity, he would include a topic that was not covered in class or in the textbook to see what the students would do. Every semester, almost all of the students would skip the question on the topic that was not covered in class, but a few of them would do the independent research it took to answer the question.

Trying to locate a pattern, the professor would ask these students where they went to high school; he discovered that most of them where homeschooled. He was fascinated by the self-initiative these students had while their classmates waited to be told what to do with the question. Over time, the professor became so impressed with homeschoolers, he left university teaching to start his own homeschool science curriculum company.

Many universities are noticing the diverse portfolios of homeschoolers. They are impressed by things like the in-depth study of a subject of the student's choosing, experience in higher education classes such as dual-credit programs, and extensive community involvement. Some universities are even actively recruiting home-educated students. The university Cooper and Cassie ended up attending offered a homeschool visitation day specifically for homeschoolers, and they really rolled out the red carpet for us.

When I was in high school, an aptitude counselor told me the one thing college students struggle with the most is time management. I was advised to schedule my long-term projects, like research papers, in small segments, and to self-reward when goals were reached. In college, I was warned, I might be given an assignment at the beginning of the semester and told the due date, without a single mention of it in between. No one would be looking over my shoulder telling me how to pace myself along the way. I would have to do that for myself. College was the first time I really had a chance to practice scholastic time management.

As I moved from my role as teacher, to tutor, to the monitor stage of educating my kids, I began to give them more freedom with their schedule so they could practice their own time management skills *before* they got to college. I gave them a week's worth of assignments; they could decide when and how they got them done as long as they were done by the end of the week. They could even reward themselves by getting done by Tuesday if they chose. We practiced getting the least desired task out of the way first so that the rest was "downhill." When my son told me he needed more structure in his daily schedule, we talked about how he could create that for himself.

Self-initiative, self-reward, and time management skills will really help a student while they're in university and beyond. These skills, among others, are what employers call "soft skills." I once heard the recruiter of a large employer speak about "What Employers Are Looking For." She said it is easier for a company to teach a new employee the "hard skills" of the job—the elements of the job description—than it is to teach them the "soft skills" like punctuality, self-motivation, problem solving, clear communication, and most importantly, people skills like conflict resolution. When given the choice, her company would hire a potential employee who exhibited a mastery of the "soft skills" every time, knowing that the hardest training had already been done. So for good measure, I included several books on people skills, like Dale Carnegie's classic *How to Win Friends and Influence People* to our homeschool reading list.

Once homeschoolers reach adulthood, a 2017 National Home Education Research Institute study has found that they:

> Participate in local community service more frequently than does the general population

> Vote and attend public meetings more frequently than the general population

> Go to and succeed at college at an equal or higher rate than the general population

> By adulthood, internalize the values and beliefs of their parents at a high rate

That last item, "internalize the values and beliefs of their parents" is worth every single minute I spent homeschooling. I have known more than a few friends who paid a small fortune to send their children to private schools that reflected their own values and beliefs, only to have a semester or two at a university tear down much of what they tried to build up.

If a student is taught *what* to think instead of *how* to think, after years of seeing teachers as ultimate authority figures, some students will simply accept what a college professor says, even if it contradicts the values of their parents. How can that be tuition money well spent?

But a homeschooling parent has the opportunity to train their students how to think critically, how to recognize faulty logic, how to debate and defend multiple positions, and to answer any of their questions at the time they come up. In the process, their child's beliefs can become more personalized and internalized and are less likely to crumble when challenged.

That said, we would do well to look beyond what kind of college our children can get into, or what kind of career they can have, to what kind of people, what kind of *adults* we want our children to be.

As I considered homeschooling, I knew the happiness in my kids' lives would be greatly impacted by the happiness in their relationships—with friends, coworkers, future spouses, and even— me.

The college graduations of Cooper and Cassie

fourteen

How Does Homeschooling Affect the Parent?

"I'd rather regret the things I've done than regret the things I haven't done."

– Lucille Ball

It was spring, my kids were still pretty young, and I was sitting in a support group meeting at my homeschool co-op. The group was recognizing graduating seniors, and the parents were telling us about their future plans. I'll never forget the mother who stood up, with her arm around her graduating daughter whom she had homeschooled from preschool through high school.

"I can't believe this time is here." she almost whispered. "I do not regret one moment I've spent with this young lady. Not one."

That. That right there was exactly how I wanted to feel one day. Whenever I have a big decision to make, I try to project myself into the future looking back at the decision and asking myself, "Did you regret doing it, or not doing it?"

For me, personally, when it came to the decision of whether to homeschool or not, I knew I would regret *not* doing it.

I definitely had some trepidation before I began. I knew that homeschooling was a big commitment of my energy and time, and that by choosing it, I would not be able to do other things—which, at the moment, escape me. I guess they weren't all that important.

I was concerned that I wasn't organized enough to homeschool. There are some homeschool moms out there who could drop everything and run a Fortune 500 company without breaking a sweat. I am not one of those moms. My attention span is short. I get easily distracted. Russ can come home and find cleaning projects halfway complete and then abandoned—a vacuum in the middle of the living room, or furniture polish and rags left on the coffee table.

I even dropped a kid off at violin lessons once *without the kid*. I saw Cassie climb into my car but didn't notice that she got out of it and went back inside the house when I stopped to chat with a neighbor in the driveway. I finished the chat, got in the car, and drove off, talking to her all the way down the street. I pulled in front her teacher's house.

"Have a good lesson!" I told her.

But when I looked in the rearview mirror, the car was empty! After her lesson, her teacher told me she's had parents who have forgotten their child's sheet music. She's had parents who have forgotten their child's instrument. But she's never had a parent who had forgotten their *child!*

And my kids got really skilled at getting me off topic during school. I knew what they were really up to, but we still had fun going down the rabbit holes of YouTube videos or some other trail together. And they loved it whenever my friend Trina would call or drop by. They would proclaim it a "Trina break!" while we visited, and they were off to enjoy some extra free time.

Yeah, I didn't exactly run the tightest of ships, but we, eventually, got where we needed to go. I didn't see myself as the captain, but as a fellow voyager who was along for the journey too.

Once my kids got a taste of a classroom, either in a dual-credit class or in a university, they each, independently, sincerely thanked me for homeschooling them. And even when they were young, at times they would express the sweetest gratitude in a little note. I saved those notes because I needed to reread them on the days I asked myself, "What in the world have I gotten myself into?"

But like a new mother who forgets all the pain of labor once she's holding her baby, I look at my three grown kids now and forget all about the days I could empathize with species that devour their own young.

There were also some unexpected perks to being a homeschool mom. For example, I enjoyed being a one-woman PTA. When we were planning a weekend camping trip with some church families, they asked me if my kids could get permission to get out of school early on a Friday.

"Let me check with their school's administration." I bowed my head, closed my eyes for a second, and then reopened them. "Permission granted," I said with a wink.

Another perk is that homeschooling makes you smarter. Remember, you can recall up to 90% of what you teach. And on top of that, think about the lack of life experience and context you had when you went through school the first time. When you teach it, and learn it again, you have a much deeper understanding of things like the world events of history and the themes in classic literature. You see things you were too young to notice before. It's exciting! And your kids pick up on that excitement, and then they get excited too.

And here's a perk I did not see coming—it's the close relationships I still have with my grown kids. They really are my best friends. I'm so pleased that they still want to spend time with me and my husband—we all just love hanging out together. I am definitely not a parent who is complaining I don't see or hear from my adult children often enough.

I guess I have to attribute this closeness to homeschooling and all the time we spent together as a family. When it came time for them to go, I honestly felt "done." My job was complete. I had left it all on the field.

Some parents begin to panic as their children grow closer to leaving the nest because they don't feel "finished" yet. They frantically try to cram in some last-minute parenting because there are so many things they wanted their kids to know, but somehow, time just got away from them.

But I didn't let time get away from us. I took the time to homeschool, and we took our time doing it. That has left me a content, guilt-free, no regrets empty nester.

What a nice surprise.

As I considered homeschooling, the last person I expected to benefit from it was— me.

A "finished" home educator enjoying her grown kids

fifteen

What Comes Next?

"Two roads diverged on a wood, and I—I took the one less traveled by, and that has made all the difference."

– Robert Frost

After I first mentioned homeschooling to my husband, and after several conversations where I tried my best to answer his questions and concerns, we came to a better understanding of each other. I was reminded that Russ is not a public school teacher because he loves the public school system—he is a teacher because he loves kids. And that was the same reason I wanted to homeschool *our* kids.

"Even though I'm not a professional teacher like you," I told him, "there's not a teacher on this planet who will love our kids like I do."

And just like that, we were on the same page. Now we knew we both wanted to teach for the same reason—we were each motivated to teach out of love.

"Okay. Let's take it year by year and see how it goes."

Fair enough.

So that's what we did. We took it year by year and ended up homeschooling all the way through high school. In the beginning, the "Let's see how it goes" approach took a lot of the pressure off. I've made several big decisions in my life by first deciding to just give something a try because I would rather look back and say, "I'm glad I did" instead of "I wish I had."

The optimal time to dip your toe into the homeschooling pool is before your kids are taught by someone else, and you are still their main authority figure. I remember hearing of a little boy whose kindergarten teacher constantly mispronounced one of the numbers. When his mother heard him mispronounce it and corrected him, he resisted because he said, "That's not the way the teacher says it." Already, the teacher, not the mother, was the final authority on the matter in his young mind.

The good news is that most parents are *natural* teachers. Have you ever seen a mom or a dad read a book to their young child? They ask their child constant questions: "Where's the cow? Can you point to the duck? What does the cat say?" They probably weren't taught to teach that way, it's just innate. If homeschooling is done from the start, it is a seamless continuation of the intuitive teaching of a parent with their own child, in the safety of their home, with a little more guided focus.

However, if your child has already experienced a classroom-style education, they can still easily adjust to homeschooling. I have met families who have removed their children from schools at all different grade levels, from elementary to high school, with great results. And I have even met kids who initiated leaving their school to be homeschooled, either due to social pressures from peers or a desire to focus more on a particular skill.

To begin, a family needs to decide who will be primarily responsible for the homeschooling, and who will be primarily responsible for earning a living. Russ and I decided to live off of one income so I could devote myself to it full-time. It was a sacrifice, but one we would gladly make again. Fortunately, with today's technology, the ability to work from home, either in full or in part, opens up the possibility of homeschooling to so many more families. Single working moms are doing it, and even families with two working parents are making it work.

Next, join a homeschool support group. It really did help to have other people in our lives who were traveling the same path. And other parents can have a wealth of information; it was another homeschool mom sitting next to me on a basketball game bleacher who told me about dual-credit classes. That one conversation saved us thousands of dollars in college tuition! You can connect with other homeschoolers through a co-op, organized sports teams, or other types of support groups. The friendships our family made with other homeschool families were invaluable.

Thankfully, homeschooling is currently legal in all fifty states, so the next step is to find out if your state has any special requirements. Some states have a few minimal stipulations, while some states have none at all. The Home School Legal Defense Association (hslda.org) is a great place to find out.

The final step is choosing a curriculum. I found this to be the most challenging part of getting started simply because there are so many great ones to choose from. Going to a homeschool convention or book fair is helpful because it gives you a chance to consult with curriculum vendors and other parents. Some curriculums are all-inclusive, and some just cover a single subject and can be mixed and matched for a truly customized approach. But there's absolutely no reason to recreate the wheel. Someone has already done the hard work for you. There are excellent curriculums available that require little to no preparation— just open the teacher's manual and go! They know it's best to require as little of you as possible so that you can spend the most amount of time with your kids.

There is this wide, well-traveled road running through the middle of our society called "The Way Things Are Done." So many people have been down this road, so many people are on this road, and so many people have championed this road, we sometimes forget to look up and ask, "Wait, *why* are we doing things this way?"

That's the same question we need to ask about "The Way We Educate Our Kids." Much of our society is on auto-pilot—heads down, moving with the flow of traffic, doing what is common, accepted, and expected. We dutifully step onto that long K–12 escalator that has no steering wheel, no brakes, and only handrails to keep us in place until we reach the end. And what exactly is at the end? Have we stopped to ask where this thing is going, or if it's the best way to get there?

Now is a great time to ask, "Why?" It's an even better time to ask, "Why not?" Why not rebel a little from what society expects? Why not tune out the experts who have never met your kids? Why not play hooky from "The Way Things Are Done?"

You might worry that homeschooling is too risky. But letting people you barely know fill your child's mind, in your absence, for twelve years, seems like the bigger risk. You might be afraid you'll ruin your child's future. But giving them an unhurried childhood, a love of learning, and the initiative to self-teach is a solid foundation for anyone's future. You might feel like you or your kids will miss out on some long-held traditions. But you won't miss out on each other.

When you start measuring time by the growth of a child, it begins to fly. The days are long, but the years are short. Don't let time just somehow get away from you. Don't be a parent who doesn't feel "done" when their child leaves home. No businessman says on their deathbed they wish they'd spent *more* time at the office. And no parent looks back and says they wish they'd spent *less* time with their kids.

You picked up this book and read it, so what comes next is up to you. I hope you've said, "I've never thought of it that way before." I hope you are now thinking outside the classroom box. And if you are leaning towards homeschooling, I hope this book is the encouragement and the friendly nudge you need to get started.

Now that you've heard my story, what will your story be?

As you consider homeschooling, remember, there's not a teacher on this planet who will love your kids more than — you!

afterword

Now that you've heard this home educator's take on homeschooling, it's time to hear from the students themselves—my three fabulous kids, and from their principal—my wonderful husband Russ.

(At the time of the writing of this Afterword, all three of our adult children are in their early to mid-twenties.)

Cooper

"You were homeschooled? But...you're so normal."

This was the response almost anytime I told someone of my schooling growing up. My impeccable social sensibilities just could not compute with their preconceived notions of homeschoolers.

I think a common misconception of homeschooling is that you virtually never leave the house, and your social interactions are limited to when you accompany your mother to the grocery store, or escort your sister to the prom in your living room. That's not quite how it was.

Now granted, I did have to be proactive with making friends. But whether it was through church, sports, or other extracurricular activities, the amount of interactions I got to have with not just my peers, but with people of differing ages, more than made up for any amount of time I spent at home. Being homeschooled meant that I got to branch out and make friends from lots of different schools and from all walks of life, not just the ones with whom I would have shared AP History.

Another misconception about homeschoolers is that they won't adjust well to college. I even wondered about that myself. But it turns out I had a big advantage over my friends: I had already had the chance to develop time management skills.

A key difference between high school and college is the newfound sense of freedom that a lot of kids haven't quite experienced before. No one's forcing you to attend class, no parent is waking you up if you're running late, and no teacher is reminding you when your assignments are due. All of that is gone.

I can't tell you how many instances I've witnessed friends wrestle mightily with staying on top of their college schoolwork. They aren't slouches, either. Some went to top prep schools, others were top of their class. Yet, time and time again, I watched as they struggled to get their work done on time. Not because they weren't smart, but because they were used to having someone telling them what to do and when to do it.

While I was in college, I actually had a professor ask me how I was making the adjustment from the highly-structured homeschool setting to the more loosely-structured college atmosphere. I just kind of laughed and said, "Have you *met* my mom?"

Trust me, it was easier for me to adjust from homeschool to university than it was for my friends to adjust from high school to university. Even though we were also loosely-structured at home, my mother did a wonderful job of giving me the time and space to learn how to time manage my own schoolwork growing up. When I told her I needed more structure, she showed me how to create it for myself: a timeline for my day, a list of things to get done, and how to motivate myself by getting things I least preferred out of the way first, and then rewarding myself with breaks when an item was completed.

If there's anything I want you to take away from this, it's that homeschooling does not, by any means, put you at a disadvantage—if anything, it's quite the opposite. I have friends who were homeschooled from K–12 that are lawyers, doctors, dentists, founders of their own companies, and yes, even professional basketball players in the NBA. I believe that homeschooling gave me all the tools necessary to succeed in life—socially, academically, and professionally.

Cassie

Homeschooling gave me two very special gifts that have served me well as I navigate life outside of my childhood home.

The first gift is initiative. I received a BBA in Entrepreneurship and a MA in International Business within five years. School, in a traditional classroom setting, was easy for me because no one had to hold my hand—I received assignments and did them without prompting or coddling. My education was my responsibility.

This initiative has also served me in my career. Just a month before I walked the stage with my undergraduate degree, my alma mater hired me to open and manage a coffee shop on campus. I ran this business virtually on my own for three years with no one looking over my shoulder, and I've just been hired to open a new coffee shop in another state. It has been the gift of initiative that homeschooling gave me that has made me a successful entrepreneur.

The second gift—my very favorite gift—is a stable and realistic relationship with my mom. In high school, once my friends and I had reached "that age"—you know, the wicked, hormonal, teenage girl age that parents dread. I remember being puzzled by the ways my friends treated their moms and spoke about them to me behind their backs. I have a very clear memory of a friend acting very disrespectful toward her mom in my presence over something very trivial.

Then it dawned on me how differently I saw my own mother. It was like my friend was predisposed to assume her mom was out to get her, and that tension snapped at the slightest provocation. I wasn't immune to hormones or outbursts, but I didn't assume that my mom was acting against my interests when she said things that rubbed me the wrong way. It was unfathomable to me that my friends couldn't recognize that their parents were on their side!

As I've grown and pondered why my perspective on my mom was so different from my friends, I've come to the conclusion that the biggest difference is in the purpose I saw my mom had in my life and how complete of a person she was to me. My friend's moms cooked for them, drove them around, and did their laundry. Their mom's roles in their lives were mostly utilitarian, so any time they did or said something that wasn't useful in their opinion, it was easy to brush them off or lash out at them for not serving them to their liking. Some of my friends were embarrassed of their moms, spoke poorly of them when they weren't around, and they showed no hesitation to talk back to them in the presence of others. I witnessed it time and time again.

The mom of a friend of mine had been a high-powered career woman before she dropped everything to have children. She poured her heart and soul into her home, serving and loving her kids. To my friend, however, there was a juxtaposition between her professional teachers informing her on current events with authority and her mother who was cooped up in their home. My friend genuinely believed that her mom was an idiot who was uninformed and out-of-date.

Conversely, my mom was an authority figure whose years of experience were not only fascinating to me but added to her credibility. I recognized that she had lived a life long before I came along, and that she brought everything she had learned into our home and our education. Through this, my mom earned my genuine respect.

However, the biggest difference of all was that, though my mom did all of those things a mother should do, she was also my friend. We would listen to music together on our way to ballet class. We would watch movies together on the weekends. We would go on Slurpee runs on hot summer days.

Because of the time we were able to spend together and the stories she told me, my mom was a real person to me. I knew the name of her first crush, I knew about the places she had traveled, I knew and shared her taste in music, I knew what she liked in her coffee . . . I knew her. And better yet, I liked her. As I've gotten older, our friendship has deepened, and I still genuinely enjoy being around her.

Nothing will ever be more valuable to me than the gift of friendship with my family. But as a daughter amongst many who have strained relationships with their moms, I'm especially grateful for what we have cultivated together. My bond with my mother is special and rare, and homeschooling gave me the time to get to know her and love her the way I do.

Catie

One of the most important things you can do in life is to learn how to love yourself. I believe homeschool gave me the perfect opportunity to do just that. Being homeschooled gave me a lot of time with my family and a lot of time on my own. Some people might think that a kid having a lot of alone time is a bad thing, but it was actually very helpful to me.

The majority of my friends attended either public or private schools. I started to notice how different my friends saw themselves compared with how I saw myself. They were worried about what other people thought of them—from how they dressed, talked, and who their groups of friends were. They were trying to "fit in" with their peers as best they could. I found myself a little bewildered at times thinking, "Why would I care about that person's opinion of me when they don't even know me?"

And because I was able to have a good amount of alone time during my school years, I became very confident in who I was. I was comfortable in my own skin, I could hear my own thoughts, and I could recognize my inner voice. I completely accepted myself for who I was. How could I not? I spent the majority of my time with my family who loved me, accepted me, and encouraged me to be the best version of myself.

Compare that with my friends who spent the majority of their day with people who were often their competitors, who made them feel inferior, or would reject them if they were different from what was considered "cool" or "popular." How can a positive self-identity be formed in that kind of environment?

Homeschool created a comfortable environment that allowed me to become exactly who I was meant to be, free from the fear of the judgment from others. Being homeschooled was one of the biggest blessings of my life.

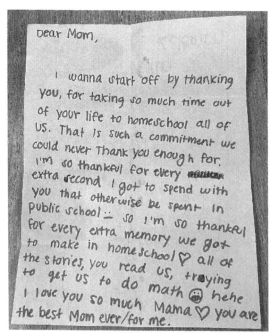

Dear Mom,

I wanna start off by thanking you, for taking so much time out of your life to homeschool all of us. That is such a commitment we could never Thank you enough for. I'm so thankful for every minute extra second I got to spend with you that otherwise be spent in public school. So I'm so thankful for every extra memory we got to make in homeschool ♥ all of the stories, you read us, traying to get us to do math 😊 hehe I love you so much Mama ♥ you are the best Mom ever/for me.

A letter Catie wrote in middle school

Russ

"You want to what?"

Yes, those were the first words out of my mouth when Cari told me she wanted to homeschool our children. And yes, all of the questions and concerns that have been discussed in this book were swimming through my mind.

As a public educator, there are things I strive to give all of my students—as much individual attention as possible, assignments that encourage a passionate participation, a desire to do their best work, and lessons that relate to life well beyond the classroom.

However, the built-in bureaucracy that comes along with institutionalized learning is often more of a hindrance than a help. Time restraints, crowded classrooms, the latest educational fads promoted by the administration, grading hoops I must jump through, and the act of congress it takes to have an activity outside of the classroom get in the way of my ability to make my classes all that I want them to be for my students.

I wish I could have the same flexibility and spontaneity Cari had with her school day—the way she could customize things to better suit our kids, the kinds of field trips they could take, and the amount of time they were able to spend outside their "classroom." There were a few times I even offered to switch places with her!

As Cari mentioned, I am a public educator because I love working with kids, and through no choice of their own, a public school is where most of the kids are. At my inner-city high school, I work with kids from a wide variety of cultural backgrounds and family situations. But in the end, kids are a lot alike regardless of where they are being educated. When it comes to learning, they can be easily distracted and difficult to motivate, and they all need a clear understanding of what's expected of them and consistent consequences when those expectations are not met.

All forms of teaching come with their own inherent challenges, but the frustrations and joys Cari experienced as a home educator were not all that different from the frustrations and joys I experience as a public school teacher. Yet, we were both working diligently to give our students the best possible foundation for their lives as adults.

Final verdict: I'm so glad I told Cari "yes" to homeschooling. Just reading what our kids have to say about her and their homeschool experience in this Afterword is the best indicator of how it turned out. Not only am I proud of what my kids have accomplished, but more importantly, I'm proud of who they have become.

Russ always says his favorite name is "Dad."

acknowledgments

Thank you to my editors:

Julie Plagens, author and blogger, momremade.com

Mark Stuertz, writer and author,

linkedin.com/in/markstuertz/

Thank you to my proof readers:

Crystal Colombo

Boone and Peggy Powell

Trina Oshman

Thank you to my photographer:

Russ Kelemen, rkelemen.zenfolio.com

And thank you to my Lord and Savior:

Jesus Christ

Resources

Chapter One
Mary Flo Ridley. Birds & Bees, birds-bees.com

Chapter Two
Dr. Bruce Wilkinson. *The Seven Laws of the Learner: How to Teach Almost Anything to Practically Anyone*, Walk Thru the Bible Ministries, 1992, walkthru.org and also, Teach Every Nation, brucewilkinsoncourses.org
Clip for the audiobook is used with permission.

Chapter Five
"Increasing Number of Parents Opting to Have Children School-Homed," The Onion, theonion.com, March 29, 2010

Ken Robinson. Transcript of the story of Gillian Lynne is from a TedTalk, ted.com, posted June 2006 and eventually included in his book, *The Element.*
Clip for the audiobook used Courtesy of TED.

Chapter Six
Dr. Howard G. Hendricks. *The Seven Laws of the Teacher,* Walk Thru the Bible Ministries, 1987, walkthru.org

National Home Education Research Institute, nheri.org

Chapter Seven
Gary Chapman. *The Five Love Languages,* Northfield Publishing, 1995

Chapter Eight
John Taylor Gatto. *Dumbing Us Down, The Hidden Curriculum of Compulsory Schooling,* New Society Publishers, 1992

Chapter Nine
The concepts of models, mental images, and stories as a way around paradigms are from Richard Maybury. *Personal, Career, and Financial Security*, Blue Stocking Press, 1994

Karen Andreola. *A Charlotte Mason Companion, Personal Reflections on the Gentle Art of Learning*, Charlotte Mason Research and Supply, 1998

Chapter Ten
John Holzmann. *William Wilberforce, God's Politician*, Sonlight Curriculum, Ltd, 1996

Ann Weil. *Red Sails to Capri*, Sonlight Curriculum, Ltd, 1952

Chapter Thirteen
National Home Education Research Institute, nheri.org

Chapter Fifteen
The Home School Legal Defense Association, hslda.org

All Scripture references are from *The Living Bible Paraphrased*, Kenneth Taylor, Tyndale Publishing, 1971

References to Cari's Curriculum Choices

Sonlight, sonlight.com

Math-U-See, mathusee.com

Sing 'n Learn, singnlearn.com